ENGLISH
PORTUGUESE

EDITORIAL ESTAMPA

Versão portuguesa: David Ferreira
Capa: José Antunes
Composição: b&f Gráficos
Impressão e acabamento: Rolo & Filhos – Artes Gráficas, Lda.
1.ª edição: Abril de 2002
Depósito legal: 181048/02
ISBN: 972-33-1756-7

Contents

Figurative Pronunciation

Portuguese pronunciation is not difficult and does not present irregularities. Our system of pronunciation is based on the comparison between sounds... and Portuguese sounds.

Being aware of the lack of exactness of this system, we have chosen to give you a simple manual within everybody's reach.

Following that, we offer you some observations that will help make the pronunciation of this language easier for you.

The alphabet

The Portuguese alphabet and vowels are the same as the English ones, with the exception of three letters: K, W and Y (KAPPA, DOUBLE YOU, IPSLON). These letters are only used in foreign words that have come into use in Portuguese.

A as in **a**pple
B as in **b**eer
C as in **s**ear
D as in **d**ear
E as in **air**
F as in **eff**
G as in **g**ear
H is mute
I as in l**i**p
J as in **j**otta
L as in **l**ove

M	as in **m**other
N	as in **n**o
O	as in h**o**t, p**o**t, h**o**p
P	as in **p**ier
Q	as in **k**ier
R	as in the sound ai**r** but using a small throat gargle at the end
S	as in **s**ound
T	as in **t**ear
U	as **oo**
V	as in **v**ere
X	as **sheesh**
Z	as in **z**ebra

Pronunciation

In the pronunciation system used in this book, Portuguese sounds are represented by spellings of the nearest possible sound in English. Therefore, read the word as if you were reading an English word. The syllable stressed is shown in bold. The following notes should help you:

	REMARKS	EXAMPLE	PRONOUNCED
a, e, o	as in f**a**ther, p**e**t, p**o**t	**pá, pé, pó**	pa, pe, po
ah, oh	as in m**a**, s**o**	**maço, dou**	**mah**-soo, door
ee, oo	as in tr**ee**, t**oo**	**triste, tudo**	treesht, **too**doo
ay	as in m**ay**	**meia**	**may**ah
eh	as in **air**	**disquete**	disk**ette**
uh	as in m**o**ther	**que**	ker
j	as in the s in lei**s**ure	**jejum**	juh-**joong**

There are a number of nasal sounds in Portuguese which, as with similar sounds in French, are pronounced by letting air out through the nose as well as the mouth:

	REMARKS	EXAMPLE	PRONOUNCED
ang	as in **an**gry	**maçã**	ma**sang**
ayng	as in m**ai**n	**homem**	**om**ayng
eeng	halfway between mean and ming	**mim**	mee
ong	as in H**o**ng Kong	**com**	kom
oong	as in s**oo**n	**algum**	al-**goong**
owng	as in t**ow**n	**tão**	towng
oyng	as in p**oi**nt	**põe**	poyng

Pronouncing Portuguese words from their spelling is not easy, as it is a ´flowing´ language in which the sounds change depending on the way in which words are joined together. The following rules will help:

	REMARKS	EXAMPLE	PRONOUNCED
ç	as in fa**c**e	**faço**	**fah**-soo
ch	as in **sh**ampoo	**champô**	sham**poh**
h	always silent	**homem**	**om**ayng
lh	like lli in mi**lli**on	**milhão**	meel-**yowng**
nh	like **gn** in the french word champa**gne**	**minha**	**mign**-ah

10

Grammar

ARTICLES

Definite Article – *The*

O (masculine singular)
A (feminine singular)
Os (masculine plural)
As (feminine plural)

Indefinite Article – *A*

Um (masculine singular)
Uma (feminine singular)
Uns (masculine plural)
Umas (feminine plural)

NOUNS

Portuguese nouns are either masculine or feminine, and their gender is shown by the words **o**, **a**, **os**, **as** and **um**, **uma**, **uns**, **umas** used before them (the article):

masculine
O/um castelo The/a castle
Os castelos / (uns) castelos
The castles / castles

feminine
A/uma mesa The/a table
As mesas / (umas) mesas
The tables / tables

masculine	*feminine*
O livro vermelho	**A saia vermelha**
(the red book)	(the red skirt)

O homem falador **A mulher faladora**
(the talkative man) (the talkative woman)

To make an adjective plural, follow the general rules given for nouns.

´My´, ´Your´, ´His´, ´Her´
These words also depend on the gender and number of the following noun and not the sex of the ´owner´.

PLURAL

Nouns ending in a vowel form the plural by adding **-s**, while those ending in a consonant usually add **-es**. The exceptions to this are words ending in an **-m** which change to **-ns** in the plural and words ending in **-l** which change to **-is** in the plural:
e.g. **hotel – hotéis.**

Note: When used after the words **a** (to), **de** (of), **em** (in) and **por** (by), the articles are contracted:

a + as = às *ash*	to the
de + um = dum *doom*	of a
em + uma = numa *noomuh*	to a
por + os = pelos *peloosh*	by the

ADJECTIVE DEGREES

Comparative of equality

as...as *tão...como*

Comparative of inferiority
less...than *menos... do que*

Comparative of superiority

more...than   *mais... do que*

Superlative

very   *muito...*

Or the adjective with the ending **-íssimo/a**
e.g. pequeno – pequeníssimo.

Superlative of inferiority

the less...   *o/a/os/as menos...*

Superlative of superiority

the most...   *o/a/os/as mais...*

PRONOUNS

Subject

I	**eu**	*ee-oo*
You	**você**	*voss-seer*
He	**ele**	*eel*
She	**ela**	*ella*
It	**ele/ela**	*eel/ella*
We	**nós**	*nosh*
You	**vocês**	*voss-seers*
They (masc.)	**eles**	*eels*
(fem.)	**elas**	*ellash*

Object

Me	**me**	*muh*
You	**o/a**	*oo/ah*
Him	**o**	*oo*
Her	**a**	*ah*

Grammar

It	**o/a**	*oo/ah*
Us	**nos**	*nosh*
You	**os/as**	*oosh/ahsh*
Them (masc.)	**os**	*oosh*
(fem.)	**as**	*ahsh*

Notes

1. Subject pronouns are not normally used except for emphasis or to avoid confusion:
   Eu **vou para Lisboa e** *ele* **vai para Coimbra.**
   I'm going to Lisbon and *he's* going to Coimbra.

2. Object pronouns are usually placed after the verb and joined with a hyphen.

   Also, in sentences beginning with ´that´ and ´who´, etc. ('subordinate clauses') the pronoun precedes the verb.

3. **Me** also = to me and **nos** = to us, but **lhe** = to him/to her/to it/to you and **lhes** = to them/to you.

4. When two pronouns are used together they are often shortened. The verb will also change spelling if it ends in **-r, -s, -z** or a nasal sound.

5. The pronoun following a preposition has the same form as the subject pronoun, except for **mim** (me) and **si** (you).

Possessive pronouns and adjectives

my/mine	*meus/s, minha/s*
your/yours	*teu/s, tua/s*
his, her	*seus/s, sua/s (dele/a)*
our/ours	*nosso/a/s*
your/yours	*vosso/a/s*
their/theirs	*seu/s, sua/s (deles/as)*

Demonstrative adjectives and pronouns

this	*este/a*
that	*esse/a*
these	*estes/estas*
those	*aqueles/aquelas*

These depend on the gender and number of the noun they represent.

Relative pronouns

who	*quem*
whom	*quem*
which	*que*
that	*que*
whose	*do/a qual dos/as quais*

Interrogative adjectives and pronouns

who	*quem*
whom	*de quem*
which	*que, qual*
that	*que, o que*
what	*como*
why	*por que*
where	*onde*
when	*quando*
how much	*quanto/a*

Indefinite pronouns

another	*outro/a*
other/s	*outros/as*
a certain	*certo/a*
certain	*certo/as*
any	*qualquer, quaisquer, algum/a, alguns, algumas*

anybody, anyone	*alguém*
anything	*qualquer coisa*
some	*algum/a, alguns, algumas*
somebody, someone	*alguém*
something	*algumas coisa*
no, none	*nenhum/a, nenhuns, nenhumas*
many	*muitos/as*
much	*muito/a*
few	*poucos/as*
a few	*pouco/a*
several	*vários*
all	*todo/a/s*
both	*ambos*

ADVERBS

Of time

today	*hoje*
yesterday	*ontem*
tomorrow	*amanhã*
yet	*já*
still	*ainda*
before	*antes*
after	*depois*
early	*cedo*
late	*tarde*
first	*em primeiro lugar*

Of place

there	*aí*
here	*aqui*
beyond	*atrás*
near	perto

Grammar

Of frequency

always	*sempre*
often	*frequentemente*
sometimes	*às vezes*
usually	*normalmente*
seldom	*raramente*

Of affirmation/denial

yes	*sim*
no	*não*
maybe	*talvez*

Of quantity

enough	*bastante*
less	*menos*
very	*muito*
only	*apenas*
little	*pouco*
too much	*demasiado*
more	*mais*
nothing	*nada*

Of manner

slowly	*lentamente*
rapidly	*rapidamente*
carefully	*cuidadosamente*
easy	*facilmente*
quickly	*depressa*
slowly	*devagar*
now	*agora*
so	*assim*
better	*melhor*

well	*bem*
together	*junto/a/s*
bad	*mal*

Many of the adverbs of manner are formed adding the ending **-mente** to the adjective.

PREPOSITIONS

at	*a*
with	*com*
against	*contra*
of	*de*
since	*desde*
while	*durante*
between	*entre*
until	*até*
to	*para*
on, over	*sobre*
under, below	*sob*
in	*em*

CONJUNCTIONS

and	*e*
or	*ou*
but	*mas*
however	*contudo*
as	*como*
when	*quando*
then	*logo*
for	*pois*
if	*se*
while	*enquanto*
because	*porque*
that	*que*

VERBS

To be (permanent) - *Ser*

INDICATIVE

	PRESENT	SIMPLE PAST	IMPERFECT TENSE
eu	sou	fui	era
tu	és	foste	eras
ele			
ela ⎤	é	foi	era
você ⎦			
nós	somos	fomos	éramos
vós	sois (*)	fostes (*)	ereis (*)
eles			
elas ⎤	são	foram	eram
vocês ⎦			

	FUTUR	CONDITIONAL	IMPERATIVE
eu	serei	seria	
tu	serás	serias	sê (tu)
ele			
ela ⎤	será	seria	seja (você)
você ⎦			
nós	seremos	seríamos	
vós	sereis (*)	seríeis (*)	
eles			
elas ⎤	serão	seriam	sejam (vocês)
vocês ⎦			

SUBJUNCTIVE

IMPERFECT		FUTUR	
se eu	fosse	quando/se eu	for
se tu	fosses	quando/se tu	fores
se ele		quando/se ele	
se ela ⎤	fosse	quando/se ela ⎤	for
se você ⎦		quando/se você ⎦	
se nós	fôssemos	quando/se nós	formos
se vós	fôsseis (*)	quando/se vós	fordes (*)
se eles		quando/se eles	
se elas ⎤	fossem	quando/se elas ⎤	forem
se vocês ⎦		quando/se vocês ⎦	

Grammar

To be (temporary) - *Estar*

INDICATIVE

	PRESENT	SIMPLE PAST	IMPERFECT TENSE
eu	estou	estive	estava
tu	estás	estiveste	estavas
ele ela você	está	esteve	estava
nós	estamos	estivemos	estávamos
vós	estais (*)	estivestes (*)	estáveis (*)
eles elas vocês	estão	estiveram	estavam

	FUTUR	CONDITIONAL	IMPERATIVE
eu	estarei	estaria	
tu	estarás	estarias	está (tu)
ele ela você	estará	estaria	esteja (você)
nós	estaremos	estaríamos	
vós	estareis (*)	estaríeis (*)	
eles elas vocês	estarão	estariam	estejam (vocês)

SUBJUNCTIVE

IMPERFECT		FUTUR	
se eu	estivesse	quando/se eu	estiver
se tu	estivesses	quando/se tu	estiveres
se ele se ela se você	estivesse	quando/se ele quando/se ela quando/se você	estiver
se nós	estivéssemos	quando/se nós	estivermos
se vós	estivésseis (*)	quando/se vós	estiverdes (*)
se eles se elas se vocês	estivessem	quando/se eles quando/se elas quando/se vocês	estiverem

20

To have - *Ter*

INDICATIVE

	PRESENT	SIMPLE PAST	IMPERFECT TENSE
eu	tenho	tive	tinha
tu	tens	tiveste	tinhas
ele ela você	tem	teve	tinha
nós	temos	tivemos	tínhamos
vós	tendes (*)	tivestes (*)	tínheis (*)
eles elas vocês	têm	tiveram	tinham

	FUTUR	**CONDITIONAL**	**IMPERATIVE**
eu	terei	teria	
tu	terás	terias	tem (tu)
ele ela você	terá	teria	tenha (você)
nós	termos	teríamos	
vós	tereis (*)	teríeis (*)	
eles elas vocês	terão	teriam	tenham (vocês)

SUBJUNCTIVE

	IMPERFECT		FUTUR
se eu	tivesse	quando/se eu	tiver
se tu	tivesses	quando/se tu	tiveres
se ele se ela se você	tivesse	quando/se ele quando/se ela quando/se você	tiverem
se nós	tivéssemos	quando/se nós	tivermos
se vós	tivésseis (*)	quando/se vós	tiverdes (*)
se eles se elas se vocês	tivessem	quando/se eles quando/se elas quando/se vocês	tiverem

Grammar

To go - *Ir*

INDICATIVE

	PRESENT	SIMPLE PAST	IMPERFECT TENSE
eu	vou	fui	ia
tu	vais	foste	ias
ele ela você	vai	foi	ia
nós	vamos	fomos	íamos
vós	ides (*)	fostes (*)	íeis (*)
eles elas vocês	vão	foram	iam

	FUTUR	CONDITIONAL	IMPERATIVE
eu	irei	iria	
tu	irás	irias	vai (tu)
ele ela você	irá	iria	vá (você)
nós	iremos	iríamos	
vós	ireis (*)	iríeis (*)	
eles elas vocês	irão	iriam	vão (vocês)

SUBJUNCTIVE

IMPERFECT		FUTUR	
se eu	fosse	quando/se eu	for
se tu	fosses	quando/se tu	fores
se ele se ela se você	fosse	quando/se ele quando/se ela quando/se você	for
se nós	fôssemos	quando/se nós	formos
se vós	fosseis (*)	quando/se vós	fordes (*)
se eles se elas se vocês	fossem	quando/se eles quando/se elas quando/se vocês	forem

Grammar

To speak, to talk - *Falar*

INDICATIVE

	PRESENT	SIMPLE PAST	IMPERFECT TENSE
eu	falo	falei	falava
tu	falas	falaste	falavas
ele ela você	fala	falou	falava
nós	falamos	falámos	falávamos
vós	falais (*)	falastes (*)	faláveis (*)
eles elas vocês	falam	falaram	falavam

	FUTUR	CONDITIONAL	IMPERATIVE
eu	falarei	falaria	
tu	falarás	falarias	fala (tu)
ele ela você	falará	falaria	fale (você)
nós	falaremos	falaríamos	
vós	falareis (*)	falaríeis (*)	
eles elas vocês	falarão	falariam	falem (vocês)

SUBJUNCTIVE

IMPERFECT		FUTUR	
se eu	falasse	quando/se eu	falar
se tu	falasses	quando/se tu	falares
se ele se ela se você	falasse	quando/se ele quando/se ela quando/se você	falar
se nós	falássemos	quando/se nós	falarmos
se vós	falásseis (*)	quando/se vós	falardes (*)
se eles se elas se vocês	falassem	quando/se eles quando/se elas quando/se vocês	falarem

Grammar

23

To eat - *Comer*

INDICATIVE

	PRESENT	SIMPLE PAST	IMPERFECT TENSE
eu	como	comi	comia
tu	comes	comeste	comias
ele ela você	come	comeu	comia
nós	comemos	comemos	comíamos
vós	comeis (*)	comestes (*)	comíeis (*)
eles elas vocês	comem	comeram	comiam

	FUTUR	CONDITIONAL	IMPERATIVE
eu	comerei	comeria	
tu	comerás	comerias	come (tu)
ele ela você	comerá	comeria	coma (você)
nós	comeremos	comeríamos	
vós	comereis (*)	comeríeis (*)	
eles elas vocês	comerão	comeriam	comam (vocês)

SUBJUNCTIVE

	IMPERFECT		FUTUR
se eu	comesse	quando/se eu	comer
se tu	comesses	quando/se tu	comeres
se ele se ela se você	comesse	quando/se ele quando/se ela quando/se você	comer
se nós	comêssemos	quando/se nós	comermos
se vós	comêsseis (*)	quando/se vós	comerdes (*)
se eles se elas se vocês	comessem	quando/se eles quando/se elas quando/se vocês	comerem

Grammar

24

To leave - *Partir*

INDICATIVE

	PRESENT	SIMPLE PAST	IMPERFECT TENSE
eu	parto	parti	partia
tu	partes	partiste	partias
ele ela você	parte	partiu	partia
nós	partimos	partimos	partíamos
vós	partis (*)	partistes (*)	partíeis (*)
eles elas vocês	partem	partiram	partiam

	FUTUR	CONDITIONAL	IMPERATIVE
eu	partirei	partiria	
tu	partirás	partirias	parte (tu)
ele ela você	partirá	partiria	parta (você)
nós	partiremos	partiríamos	
vós	partireis (*)	partiríeis (*)	
eles elas vocês	partirão	partiriam	partam (vocês)

SUBJUNCTIVE

	IMPERFECT		FUTUR
se eu	partisse	quando/se eu	partir
se tu	partisses	quando/se tu	partires
se ele se ela se você	partisse	quando/se ele quando/se ela quando/se você	partir
se nós	partíssemos	quando/se nós	partirmos
se vós	partísseis (*)	quando/se vós	partirdes (*)
se eles se elas se vocês	partissem	quando/se eles quando/se elas quando/se vocês	partirem

Grammar

INDICATIVE MOOD
PRESENT

	To say/ /Dizer	To want/ /Querer	May and can/ /Poder
eu	digo	quero	posso
tu	dizes	queres	podes
ele ela você	diz	quer	pode
nós	dizemos	queremos	podemos
vós	dizeis (*)	quereis (*)	podeis (*)
eles elas vocês	dizem	querem	podem

	To read/ /Ler	To watch/ /Ver	To know/ /Saber
eu	leio	vejo	sei
tu	lês	vês	sabes
ele ela você	lê	vê	sabe
nós	lemos	vemos	sabemos
vós	ledes (*)	vedes (*)	sabeis (*)
eles elas vocês	lêem	vêem	sabem

there is/are   *há*

there was/were   *houve/havia*

(*) Not very used.

Grammar

1. Commonly used terms, phrases and expressions

1.1. Phrases of etiquette

English	Portuguese	Pronunciation
Good morning, good afternoon, good evening.	*Bom dia, boa tarde, boa noite.*	*Bon deea, boa tard, boa noyt.*
See you later, tomorrow, soon, in a bit.	*Até logo, amanhã, breve, já.*	*At-air log, amanang, brev, ja.*
Hello, goodbye.	*Olá, adeus.*	*Olar, adeer-oosh.*
Welcome.	*Bem-vindo.*	*Baine veen-doo.*
Have a good trip.	*Tenha uma boa viagem.*	*Taygna ooma boa vee-ar-jane.*
Have you had a good trip?	*Fez uma boa viagem?*	*Fearsh ooma boa vee-ar-jane?*
Yes, thank you.	*Sim, obrigado.*	*Singh, obreegardoo.*
Let me introduce you to Mr. Mrs....	*Apresento-lhe o senhor..., a senhora...*	*Apre-zen-too ller ooh segnor, a segnora...*
It's nice to meet you. How are you?	*Prazer em conhecê-lo. Como está?*	*Prar-zer em cognessair-lo. Como shtá?*
What is your name? How old are you?	*Como se chama? Que idade tem?*	*Komo-ser shama? Ker eedard tayng?*

Very well, thank you, and you?	*Muito bem, obrigado, e você?*	*Moitoo bain obreegardoo, ee vor-sear?*
My name is...	*Chamo-me...*	*Sham-moo mer....*
Please, thank you, you're welcome.	*Por favor, obrigado, não tem de quê.*	*Poor favor, obreegardoo, now tayng the kier.*
You're very kind.	*É muito amável.*	*Air mooito amar-vel.*
Please don't concern yourself with...	*Não se incomode com...*	*Nowng ser in-koo-mod com...*
It's no bother, I'm glad to do it.	*Não incomoda nada, tenho muito gosto.*	*Nowng in-koo-moda narda, tay-gnoo mooito goosh-too.*
I'm very sorry.	*Sinto muito.*	*Seen-too mooito.*
I agree with you.	*Concordo consigo.*	*Concordoo con-see-goo.*
Whenever/however you like.	*Quando, como quiser.*	*Kwandoo, comoo Kee-zeer.*
I'm very happy, I'm very comfortable here.	*Estou muito satisfeito, sinto-me muito bem aqui.*	*Esh-tour mooito sateesh-fay-too, seen-too mer mooito bain a-key.*
Pardon me, excuse me....	*Perdão...*	*Per-downg...*
I'm sorry to bother you.	*Lamento incomodar.*	*Lamentoo een-koo-moo-dar*
I'm afraid it will not be possible.	*Parece-me que não será possível.*	*Pa-ress-ser mer ker nowng se-rah poo-see-vel.*

1.2. Common phrases

Why?	*Porquê?*	*Por-kaie?*
How much?	*Quanto custa?*	*Kwantoo koosh-tar?*
Yes, no, never, never, I don't know.	*Sim, não, nunca, jamais, não sei.*	*Singh, nowng, noon-kar jar mysh, nowng say.*
Impossible.	*Impossível.*	*Im-poo-see-vel.*
Possible.	*Possível.*	*Poo-see-vel.*
A lot, nothing, a little.	*Muito, nada, pouco.*	*Mooito, narda, poorkoo.*
Can you help me, please?	*Pode ajudar-me, por favor?*	*Pod ajoo-dar mer, por favor?*
Can you tell me...?	*Pode dizer-me...?*	*Pod dee-zeer mer?...*
Do you speak English, French, Italian, German, Spanish, Portuguese?	*Fala inglês, francês, italiano, alemão, português?*	*Far-la Engleaesh, Fran-searsh, Italiano, Ala-mowng, Poor-too-gearsh?*
Can you give me...?	*Pode dar-me...?*	*Pod darm-er....?*
What would you like?	*O que deseja?*	*Ooh ker de-zay-jar?*

What can I do for you?	*Em que posso ajudá-lo?*	*Ayng ker poss-oo ajoo-dar-loo?...*
What does this, that mean?	*O que significa isto, aquilo?*	*Ooh ker seeg nee-fi-car ishtoo, akee-loo?*
Are you sure?	*Tem a certeza?*	*Tayng er ser-tear-zar?*
I'm sure, very sure.	*Tenho a certeza absoluta.*	*Tay-gnooh er ser-tear-zar absoloo-ta.*
Thank you for the information.	*Obrigado pela informação.*	*Obreegardoo pela informa-sowng.*
Call me on the telephone.	*Telefone-me.*	*Telefon-mer.*
It doesn't matter.	*Não tem importância.*	*Nowng tayng impor-tan-ceea.*
It's important.	*É importante.*	*Air import-ant.*
Please, wait a moment.	*Espere um momento, por favor.*	*Esh-pair um momen-too por favor.*
Do you understand me well?	*Compreende-me bem?*	*Comprear-ender mer bayng?*
Yes, I understand you.	*Sim, compreendo-o.*	*Singh, comprear-endoo-o.*
I don't understand you, please speak more slowly.	*Não estou a compreendê-lo, fale um pouco mais devagar, por favor.*	*Nowng eshtour a compre-en-dear-loo. Far ler oom poucoo mysh der- va- gar, Poor favor.*

I'm lost, how can I get out of here, get to...?	*Perdi-me. Como posso sair daqui, chegar a...?*	*Per-deem. Comoo possoo saeer the key, Shergar er...?*
Listen to me! Hear me out!	*Escute! Oiça!*	*Eshcoot! Oyssa!*
I'm listening.	*Estou a ouvir.*	*Esh tour er or-vear.*
In a hurry.	*Depressa.*	*Der-pressa.*
Urgent.	*Urgente.*	*Oorgente.*
Help!	*Socorro!*	*Soocor-roo!*
Help me, help us.	*Ajude-me, ajude-nos!*	*Er- jew the-mer, Er- jew the-noosh!*
Call a...	*Chamem um, uma...*	*Sham-ayng oom, Ooma...*
I would like to make a formal complaint against, for...	*Desejo apresentar uma denúncia contra, por...*	*The-zay-joo er- pre-zen-tar ooma The-nooncia contra, poor...*
I have been robbed.	*Fui roubado.*	*Fooee roh-bado.*
I have to make an urgent call.	*Tenho de fazer uma chamada urgente.*	*Tay-gnhoo the fer--zeer ooma sshamahda oorgente.*
Follow me.	*Siga-me!*	*Siga-mer!*
I would like, we would like...	*Queria, queríamos...*	*Kria, kri-amoosh...*

Horrible.	*Horrível.*	*Orree-vel.*
What a pity!	*Que pena!*	*Ker pier-nar!*
How ugly!	*Que feio!*	*Ker fay-oo!*
How pretty!	*Que bonito!*	*Ker boonitoo!*
Unfortunately.	*Infelizmente.*	*In-feleez-ment.*
Fortunately.	*Felizmente.*	*Feleez-ment.*
How interesting!	*Que interessante!*	*Ker inter-ress-unt!*
How lucky!	*Que sorte!*	*Ker sort!*
What bad luck.	*Que azar!*	*Ker azar!*

1.3. Signs and notices

For rent	*Aluga-se*	*Er loo-guesse*
Stop!	*Stop, alto!*	*Stop, altoo!*
Beware!	*Atenção!*	*Aten sowng!*
Danger.	*Perigo*	*Pereegoo*
Beware of the dog	*Cuidado com o cão*	*Kui-da-doo con oo cowng*
Go ahead	*Entrem*	*En-train*
Tourist office	*Posto de turismo*	*Posh-too the too-res-moo*
Customs	*Alfândega*	*Al- fan-the-ga*

Airport	*Aeroporto*	*Air- oo- portoo*
Train station	*Estação de caminhos-de-ferro*	*Ersh- ta-sowng the Camee-gnoosh the fair-roo*
Bus stop	*Paragem de autocarros*	*Pa-ra-jane the auto-carroosh*
Taxi stop	*Paragem de táxis*	*Pa-ra-jane the taxis*
Do not...	*Proibido*	*Proee-bee-doo*
Close the door	*Feche a porta*	*Faysh er porta*
Close for Holidays / vacation, reparations, rest	*Encerrado para férias, obras, descanso*	*En ser-radoo para fair-ee-ersh, obrush, Desh-can-sue*
No vacancy	*Completo*	*Com-plair-too*
Luggage deposit (left luggage)	*Depósito de bagagens*	*Depositoo the bagaan-jane*
Toilets, restrooms, women, men	*Lavabos de senhoras, de homens*	*Lava-boosh the segnorash, the ohmains*
Information	*Informações*	*In-for-mass-oynsh*
Reception	*Recepção*	*Rer-cep-sowng*
Detour/Diversion	*Desvio*	*Desh-vee-oo*
No way through, bathing, hunting, fishing	*Proibida a passagem, tomar banho, caçar, pescar*	*Proee-bee-dar er pas-ar-jane, tour-mar-baing- nhoo, Kass-ar, pesh-car*

Do not litter	*Proibido deitar lixo*	*Proee-bee-doo day-tar lee-shoo*
No smoking	*Proibido fumar*	*Proee-bee-doo foo-mar*
Do not feed the animals	*Proibido dar comida aos animais*	*Proee-bee-doo dar cor-me-dar owsh ani-mysh*
No camping	*Proibido acampar*	*Proee-bee-doo acamp-ar*
No minors allowed	*Proibida a entrada a menores*	*Prou-bee-dar er en-tra-da er mer-nores*
Smoking area	*Zona de fumadores*	*Zonah the foo-ma-doresh*
Parking	*Estacionamento*	*Ersh-ta-ceena-men-too*
Parking	*Parqueamento*	*Park-er-men-too*
Entrance	*Entrada*	*En-tra-da*
Exit	*Saída*	*Ser-eeda*
Emergency exit	*Saída de emergência*	*Ser-eeda the er-mer-gen-ceea*
Arrivals	*Chegada*	*She-gar-da*
Sold out	*Esgotado*	*Ersh-gor-tar-doo*

Out of service	*Fora de serviço*	*For-ra the ser-vee-sue*
Free admission	*Entrada livre*	*En-trar-da lee-vre*
For sale	*Vende-se*	*Ven-the-sser*
Do not disturb	*Não incomodar*	*Nowng incoomoodar*
Do not speak to the driver	*Não falar com o condutor*	*Nowng far-la con oo con- doo-tour*
Do not touch	*Não tocar*	*Nowng too-car*
Busy	*Ocupado*	*Ohcoo-par-doo*
Toll	*Portagem*	*Poort-ar-jane*
Crosswalk	*Passadeira*	*Passer-dayra*
Private property	*Propriedade privada*	*Proop-prees-er-dar-the pree-var-da*
Residents only	*Só para residentes*	*Sore para resi-dent-ersh*
Waiting room	*Sala de espera*	*Sa-la the ersh-pair-ra*
Sales	*Saldos*	*Sal-doosh*
Dressing room	*Vestiário*	*Vesh-tee-ar-ee-oo.*
Ring the bell	*Tocar a campainha*	*To-ca er campa-ee-gna*

1.4. Family and friends

Have you met my friends?	*Conhece os meus amigos?*	*Coogn-yes oosh meoosh ame-goosh?*
Have you met my girlfriend?	*Conhece a minha namorada?*	*Cogn-yes er meegna namor-rada?*
Let me introduce you to my brothers and their children.	*Apresento-lhe os meus irmãos e os seus filhos.*	*Apres-ent-to ller oosh me-oosh ear-mowngoosh ee oos me-oosh fee-loosh.*
How is your wife?	*Como está a sua mulher?*	*Como eshta a sewer moollyair?*
Are you married?	*É casado/a?*	*Air ker-zar-do/a?*
No, I'm single.	*Não, sou solteiro/a.*	*Nowng, sore sol-tair-oo/a*
My father, my mother and my grandparents live with me.	*O meu pai, a minha mãe e os meus avós vivem comigo.*	*Or meoo pie, a meegna may e oos me-oosh er-vohsh Vee-vain co-mee-goo.*
How many children do you have?	*Quantos filhos tem?*	*Kwantoosh fee-lhoosh tayng?*
I have two sons and one daughter, my daughter is the youngest.	*Tenho dois filhos e uma filha, a minha filha é a mais nova.*	*Tay-gnoo doysh fee-lhoosh e ooma fee-lha, er meegna fee-lha air er mysh nov-er.*
Have you come by yourself to...?	*Veio sozinho para...?*	*Vay-oo saw-zee-gnoo para....?*

| No, I have come to see some relatives, with my son. | *Não, vim ver alguns familiares com o meu filho.* | *Nowng veem vere al-goones fam-ee-lee-arsh con oo meoo feellioo.* |

| Have you been married long? | *Há muito tempo que estão casados?* | *Are moitoo ten-poo ker esh-towng ker-zar-doosh?* |

| Do you want to get a drink, to see a movie, tonight? | *Vens tomar um copo, ao cinema, esta noite?* | *Vain-esh too-mar oom co-poo, aw cinema, eshta noyt?* |

| Can I bring a friend, my cousin, my sister? | *Posso levar um amigo, a minha prima, a minha irmã?* | *Possoo ler-var oom a-mee-goo, er mee-gna pree-ma, er mee-gna ear-maan?* |

| I would love to, but tonight I want to rest from my trip. How about tomorrow? | *Gostaria muito, mas esta noite quero descansar da viagem. Por que não amanhã?* | *Gosh-ta-reea moitoo, mash esh-ta noyt care-roo desh-can-sar der vee-ar-jane. Poor kier nowng ama-gnang?* |

| Would you like to have dinner with me? | *Posso convidá-lo/a para jantar?* | *Possoo con-vee-dar-lo/a para jan-tar?* |

| I would like to see you tomorrow. | *Gostaria de a/o voltar a/o ver amanhã.* | *Gosh-ta-ria der a/o Vol-tar er vere ama-gnang.* |

| Do you mind if I sit here? | *Importa-se que me sente aqui?* | *Im-port-ass ker me sen-te a-key?* |

Are you waiting for someone?	*Está à espera de alguém?*	*Esh- tar are esh pera der al-gain?*
May I go with you to your hotel?	*Posso fazer-lhe companhia até ao hotel?*	*Possoo fa-zer-lle con-paignee-a at-air ow hotel?*
I'll pick you up at the hotel.	*Irei buscá-la/o ao hotel.*	*Ear-ray boosh-car-la/o ow hotel.*
Where can we meet?	*Onde nos podemos encontrar?*	*Ond noosh poo-der-moosh en-con-tra-r?*

Vocabulary

acquaintance	*conhecido*	*coogne-seedoo*
aunt	*tia*	*tee-ah*
brother	*irmão*	*ear-mowng*
brother-in-law	*cunhado*	*cugnardoo*
child	*criança*	*cree-an-sar*
cousin	*primo*	*pree-moo*
darling	*querido*	*keree-doo*
date, appointment	*encontro*	*encontroo*
daughter	*filha*	*fee-lleea*
daughter-in-law	*nora*	*nora*

divorced	*divorciado*	*deevors-yardoo*
family	*família*	*familiar*
father	*pai*	*pie*
father-in-law	*sogro*	*sogroo*
friend	*amigo*	*amme-goo*
friendship	*amizade*	*amee-zad*
girlfriend	*namorada*	*namoo-rada*
grandfather	*avô*	*avoo*
grandmother	*avó*	*a-voh*
grandson	*neto*	*nettoo*
husband	*marido*	*ma-reedoo*
invitation	*convite*	*con-veet*
kiss	*beijo*	*bay-joo*
love	*amor*	*amohr*
Miss	*senhorita*	*segnorita*
(misses) Mrs.	*senhora*	*segnora*
(mister) Mr.	*senhor*	*segnor*
mother	*mãe*	*mayng*
mother-in-law	*sogra*	*soh-gra*

nephew	*sobrinho*	*soo-bree-gnoo*
nice	*simpático*	*simpar-tea-coo*
niece	*sobrinha*	*soo-bree-gnah*
older	*mais velho*	*mysh vair-llo*
relationship	*relação*	*rer-la-sowng*
relative	*parente*	*par-rent*
sister	*irmã*	*ear-maang*
son	*filho*	*fee-llo*
son-in-law	*genro*	*gen-roo*
to get married	*casar-se*	*ca-zar-sse*
uncle	*tio*	*tee-oo*
widow	*viúva*	*view-va*
widower	*viúvo*	*veeoo-voo*
wife	*mulher*	*moollair*
younger	*mais novo*	*mysh norvo*

2. Travel

2.1. Travel agency

I would like to make a reservation for two plane tickets to / for...	*Desejo reservar dois bilhetes de avião para...*	*De-zay-joo re-zer-var doysh bee-llets der a-vee-owng para...*
Do you have package tours for one / two / three weeks to / for...?	*Têm viagens organizadas de uma, duas, três, semanas para...?*	*Tayng vee-are-janes or-ga-nee zar-dash de ooma, dooash, treash, se-ma-nash para...?*
How much is the price of the fare per person?	*Qual é o preço da viagem por pessoa?*	*Kwal air oo prer-soo der vee-are-jane poor pe-sso-a?*
What form of payment can I use?	*Que modos de pagamento posso utilizar?*	*Ker mo-doosh der paga-mentoo pos-soo oo- tee-lee-zar?*
I would like you to make a reservation in hotels of three, four, stars.	*Desejo que me reservem alojamento em hotéis de três, quatro, estrelas.*	*De-zay-joo ker mer re- zer-vem a-loo-ja-mem-too ayng hot-eish der treash, quatro esh-tre-lash.*
I would like to rent an apartment ocean side.	*Desejo alugar um apartamento à beira-mar.*	*De-zay-joo a-loo-gar oom apart- er-men-too are bay-ra mar.*
I would like to confirm, cancel, my flight reservation, my ticket...	*Quero confirmar, cancelar, o meu voo, reserva, bilhete...*	*Kairroo con-feer-mar, can-cer-lar, oo meoo voor, re-zer-var, bee-llet...*

41

I will be here for fifteen days.	*Permanecerei cá durante quinze dias.*	*Per-ma-ner-cer-ray car doo-rant keynz dee-ash.*
Please, the entry visa, the stay visa, the exit visa.	*Por favor, o visto de entrada, permanência, saída.*	*Poor favor oo veesh-too der en-tra der per-ma-nen-cia, sa-ee-da.*
Personal documents / vehicle documents	*Documentação pessoal, do veículo.*	*Do- coo-menta-sowng per-soo-al, doo vay-ee-coo-loo.*

Vocabulary

diuties	*taxas alfandegárias*	*Tar-shash al-fan-der-gar-ree-ash*
driver's license	*carta de condução*	*Car-ta der con-doo-sowng*
duties	*direitos alfandegários*	*Dee-ray-toosh al-fan-der-gar-ree-oosh*
luggage, baggage	*bagagem*	*Ba-gar-jane*
nacionality	*nacionalidade*	*Na-see-oo-na- lee-dar-der*
name and last name, surname	*nome e apelido*	*Nome ee aper-lee-doo*
police	*polícia*	*Poo-lee-ceear*
taxes	*taxas*	*Tar-shash*

2.3. Money

2.3.1. Banks and money exchange

Could you please tell me where is there a bank?	*Por favor, pode indicar-me onde existe uma agência bancária?*	*Poor favor pod in-dee-car-mer on-the ezeesh-ter ooma agen-cia banck-areea?*
Where can I change money?	*Onde posso cambiar moeda?*	*Ond possoo cam-bee-ar moo-air-da?*
Where is there a cash machine?	*Onde há um multibanco?*	*Ond are oom multi-bancoo?*
Could you change these dollars for local currency?	*Pode cambiar estes dólares em moeda local?*	*Pode cam-beear esh-tesh dollars ain moo-eda loo-carl?*
What is the exchange rate today?	*A quanto está hoje o câmbio?*	*A kwantoo esh-tar hoje oo cam-bee-oo?*
What is the exchange rate for the dollar, the pound, the euro?	*Qual é o valor do dólar, da libra, do euro?*	*Kual air oo va-lor do dohlar, the libra, do euroh?*
Could you give me large bills, small bills, coins...?	*Poderia dar-me notas grandes, pequenas, moedas...?*	*Poo-der-ria dar-me notash gran-desh pe-que-nash, mooer-dash...?*
I would like to know if I have received a transfer to my account for...	*Queria saber se recebi uma transferência na minha conta, no montante de...*	*Ke-ree-a sa-bear se rece-bee ooma trans-fer-ren-cia ner mee-gna con-ta, noo mon-tan-te the...*

Your balance is at zero.	*O seu saldo está a zero.*	*Oo seeo saldoo esh-tar er zairo.*
I would like to open an account in this bank.	*Pretendia abrir uma conta neste banco.*	*Pre-ten-dear a-breer ooma com-ta near-shter ban-coo.*
I would like to close my account.	*Quero cancelar a minha conta.*	*Kairoo can-cer-lar er mee-gna con-ta.*
Can I cash this cheque?	*Posso levantar este cheque?*	*Possoo le-van-tar esh-ter sheq?*
Could you tell me how much cash is available in my account?	*Pode indicar-me o saldo disponível na minha conta?*	*Pod in-dee-car-me oo saldoo deesh-poo- nee-vel na mee-gna con-ta?*
You have a negative balance.	*Você está com um saldo negativo.*	*Voss air esh-tar con oom saldoo nega-tee-voo.*
I would like to make a transfer, a deposit, to account number... for...	*Quero fazer uma transferência, um depósito, na conta número... de...*	*Kairoo fa-zer ooma trans-fe-ren-cia, oomm depositoo na con-ta noomeroo... the...*
I would like to deposit this cheque in my account.	*Quero depositar este cheque na minha conta.*	*Kairoo de-po-sitar esh ter sheq na min-gha con-ta.*
Can I change these travellers cheques?	*Posso cambiar estes cheques de viagem?*	*Possoo cam-bee-ar esh-tesh sheks the vee-are-jane?*

Could you leave me your identification document, your passport?	*Pode deixar-me o seu bilhete de identidade, passaporte?*	*Pod day-sharme oo seoo bee-lhete the ee-den-tee-dade, pass-a port?*
I have lost my credit card.	*Perdi o meu cartão de crédito.*	*Per-dee oo meoo cartao the cre-dee too.*
Please, go to the teller.	*Passe pela caixa, por favor.*	*Passe pe-la kyshar, poor favor.*
Please, sign here.	*Assine aqui, por favor.*	*Aseen-akey, poor favor.*

Vocabulary

bank	*banco*	*bancoo*
bank counter, ticket window	*caixa*	*kyshar*
bill	*nota*	*nota*
bill of exchange	*letra de câmbio*	*lea-tra the cam-beoo*
cash	*cobrança em dinheiro*	*coo-bran-saa ayng dee-gnay-roo*
cash payment	*pagamento em dinheiro*	*paga-men-too ayng dee-gnay-roo*
cheque book	*livro de cheques*	*lee-vroo the sheqs*
credit	*crédito*	*cre-dee-too*
currency	*divisa*	*dee-vee-za*
currency	*moeda*	*mooeda*

debtor	*devedor*	*de-ve-dor*
deposit	*depósito*	*de-posee-too*
discount	*desconto*	*desh-con-too*
document	*documento*	*do-coo-men-too*
expenditures, expenses	*gastos, despesas*	*gash-toosh, deshpehzash*
imprint	*impresso*	*im-pressoo*
interest	*juro*	*jooroo*
investment	*investimento*	*invesh-tee-men-too*
loan	*empréstimo*	*em-presh-tee-moo*
mortgage	*hipoteca*	*hipo-teca*
national currency	*moeda nacional*	*mooeda na-see-oo-nal*
out of circulation	*fora de circulação*	*fo-ra the cir-coo-la-sowng*
overdue	*vencimento*	*ven- seemen-too*
percentage	*percentagem*	*per-cen-ta-jane*
receipt, invoice	*factura*	*fat-oo-ra*
refund	*reembolso*	*ree-en-bolsoo*
saving	*poupança*	*por-pan-sa*
security deposit box	*cofre de segurança*	*co-fre the segoo-ransa*
stocks	*acções*	*assoynsh*
transfer	*transferência*	*trans- fe-ren-cia*

2.4. Automobiles

2.4.1. Rent a car

I would like to rent a car, with a driver, without a driver.	*Queria alugar um automóvel, com motorista, sem motorista.*	*Kria a-loogar oom auto-movel, con moto-reesh-ta, sain moto-reesh-ta.*
What cars do you have available?	*Que automóveis tem disponíveis?*	*Ker auto-moveish tayng dees-poo-nee-vayeesh?*
How much is the car rental per day and per kilometre?	*Quanto custa o aluguer por dia, e por quilómetro?*	*Kwantoo coosta oo a-loo-gair poor dear, ee poor kilom-etroo?*
And for a weekend?	*E por um fim-de-semana?*	*Ee poor oomm feen the semana?*
Is the insurance included?	*Está incluído o seguro?*	*Esh-tar in-clue-eedoo oo segoo-roo?*
When can I pick it up?	*Quando posso vir buscá-lo?*	*Kwandoo possoo veer boosh-car-loo?*
Do I need to leave a deposit?	*É necessário algum tipo de fiança?*	*Air ne-sse-sa- ree-oo al-goom tee-poo the fee-an-ssa?*
Is the documentation in the car?	*A documentação está no carro?*	*A docoo-men-ta-sowng esh-tar noo carroo?*
Do you have a branch in the city...? Could I leave the car there when I get there?	*Têm alguma sucursal na cidade...? Posso deixar lá o carro quando chegar?*	*Tayng al-goo-ma soo-coor-sal na see-dade...? Possoo day-shar lar oo carroo kwandoo she-gar?*

2.4.2. The road

Could you tell me where is the highway, the main road of the city...?	*Pode indicar-me a direcção para a auto-estrada, a estrada da cidade...?*	*Pod indee-car-me er deereh-sowng para a auto esh-trada....?*
How many kilometres away is...?	*A quantos quilómetros fica...?*	*Er kwan-toosh kilo-metroosh fee-car...?*
Is this the road to the station, airport...?	*É esta a estrada para ir para a estação, aeroporto...?*	*Air esh-tar a esh-trada para eer para er eshtar-sowng, airoportoo...?*
You are on the wrong road.	*Enganou-se na estrada.*	*Enga-nou-sser ner eshtra-dar.*
Go back where you came from, you are going the opposite way.	*Volte para trás, está a ir no sentido contrário.*	*Volt para trás eshtar er eer noo sentee-doo contra-reeoo.*
Go straight ahead until you reach the square.	*Siga sempre em frente até chegar à praça.*	*See-gar sen-pre en fren-ter etair sher-gar are pra-ssa.*
Turn to the left, the right.	*Vire à esquerda, à direita.*	*Vee-re are esh-kier-da, are dee-ray-tar.*
Is it a good road?	*A estrada é boa?*	*Er esh-trada air boa?*
Is it dangerous?	*É perigosa?*	*Air pree-goza?*
Go to the first intersection.	*Vá até ao primeiro cruzamento.*	*Var a-tair ow pree mayroo crooza-mentoo.*

Could you show me on this map where we are?	Pode assinalar-me neste mapa o local onde estamos?	Pod asee-na-lar-mer neshter mapa oo loo-cal ond eshta-moosh?
Which is the best road, the shortest, the most interesting, the quickest, to go to...?	Qual é o melhor caminho, o mais curto, o mais interessante, o mais rápido, para ir para...?	Kual air oo mer-lhor carmee-gnoo, oo mysh coor-too, oo mysh inter-rerssan-ter, oo mysh ra-pee-doo, para eer para...?
Is there a city nearby? A hotel? A place where I can spend the night?	Há alguma cidade perto? Algum hotel? Algum sítio onde passar a noite?	Are al-gooma see-darde pair-too? Al-goom hotel? Al-goom seetee-oo onder per-ssar er noyt?
Where is the nearest gas station?	A que distância fica a bomba de gasolina mais próxima?	Er ker dees-tancia fee-car er bom-ber the ger-zoolee-ner mysh pro-seemer?
Can I get to the city centre by car?	Posso ir de carro até ao centro da cidade?	Poss eer the car-rroo er-tair ow cen-troo the see-darde?

2.4.3. Traffic police

Let me see your proof of insurance and your driver's license.	Mostre-me os documentos do carro e a carta de condução.	Mosh-tremer osh docoo-mentoosh doo car-rroo ee er carter the con-doosowng.
Here is my documentation.	Aqui tem os documentos.	A-key tain osh docoo-mentoosh.
I have to give you a ticket, make a report.	Tenho de lhe passar uma multa, denunciá-lo.	Tay-gnoo the lle persar ooma mool-tar, the noon-see-areloo.

I would like to know the reason.	*Queria saber o motivo.*	*Kria ser-bear oo moo teevoo.*
You were driving over the speed limit.	*Você circulava a grande velocidade.*	*Vorsear seer-coolar-ver er grande ver-loo-seedar-der.*
You have overlooked a traffic signal.	*Você desrespeitou um sinal de trânsito.*	*Vorsear deshresh-paytour oom see-nal the transito.*
You didn't stop in front of the stop sign.	*Não parou no sinal de stop.*	*Nowng pa-rou noo see-nal the stop.*
Would you open the trunk of the car?	*Pode abrir a mala do carro?*	*Pod er-breer er mar-la doo carroo?*
I didn't realize I was going so fast.	*Não me apercebi de que ia com tanta velocidade.*	*Nowng me er-perser-bee the ker-ee-er con tantar ver-loo-seedarde.*
I didn't see the sign.	*Não vi bem a sinalização.*	*Nowng vee bain a seener-lee-zassao.*
How much is the fine?	*Em quanto fica a multa?*	*Ayng kwantoo fee-ca a moolta?*
Please, sign here.	*Assine aqui, por favor.*	*Asseen akey, poor favor.*
Get out of the car!	*Saia do carro!*	*Sya doo carroo.*
Stay inside the car!	*Permaneça dentro do carro!*	*Permaner-ssa den-troo doo carroo!*
Drive carefully.	*Circule com precaução.*	*Seercool con precow-sowng.*

2.4.4. Service station

Where can I find a service station?	*Onde há uma estação de serviço?*	*Ond eshtar ooma eshta-sowng the ser-veessoo?*
How far is the next gas / petrol station?	*A que distância fica a próxima bomba de gasolina?*	*A ker deesh-tancia fee-ca a pros-eema bom-ber the gazo-lina?*
How much is a litre of gas / petrol?	*Qual é o preço do litro de gasolina?*	*Kwal air oo preer-ssoo doo leetroo the gazo-lina?*
I would like to fill up, fill up the tank, please.	*Quero atestar, encha o depósito, por favor.*	*Kerro atesh-tar, ensha oo depo-zeetoo, poor favor.*
I'd like... litres of gas / petrol.	*Queria... litros de gasolina.*	*Kria... lee-troosh the gazo-lina.*
I would like a can of oil.	*Dê-me uma lata de óleo.*	*Dear mer ooma lata the oleo.*
Check the oil level.	*Verifique-me o nível do óleo.*	*Veree-fee-que mer oo nee-vel do oleo.*
Can you check the tyre pressures?	*Poderia verificar a pressão dos pneus?*	*Poode-rear veree-fee-car a pre-sowng doosh pneosh?*
Can you check the brakes?	*Poderia verificar os travões?*	*Poode-rear veree-fee-car oosh travoesh?*
Could you please fill the radiator with water?	*Por favor, poderia pôr água no radiador?*	*Poor favor, poodea-reea por arg-ua noo rar-deeador?*

The windscreen / windshield wiper do'nt work.	*O limpa-pára-brisas não funciona.*	*Oo limpa para bree-zas nowng foon-sseona.*
I would like to wash the car.	*Queria lavar o carro.*	*Kria lavar oo carroo.*
No, thank you, it's not necessary.	*Não, não é necessário, obrigado.*	*Nowng, nowng air nesse-ssario, obri-gardoo.*

2.4.5. Service station (repairs)

How can I call a tow truck to take the car to the repair shop?	*Como poderei chamar um reboque que me leve o carro à oficina?*	*Comoo poo-deray shamar oom rer-bock ker mer lairve oo carroo are ofee-seena?*
Where is there a repair shop?	*Onde é que existe uma oficina de reparações?*	*Ond air ker ezeesh-ter ooma ofee-seena the repar-ra-ssoynsh?*
Could you tow my car, please?	*Por favor, pode rebocar o carro?*	*Poor favor, pod rer-boccar oo carroo?*
How far is the nearest repair shop?	*A que distância fica a oficina mais próxima?*	*A ker deesh-tancia fee-ca a ofee-seena mysh pro-seema?*
The battery is dead.	*A bateria está descarregada.*	*A bateria eshtar deshca-rer-garda.*
There's something wrong with the engine. It's making a strange sound.	*Há uma avaria no motor. Ouve-se um ruído estranho.*	*Are ooma avaria noo mootor. Orve-sser oom roo-eedoo esh-tray-gnoo.*

Could you give me an estimate?	*Pode fazer-me um orçamento?*	*Pod fazer mer oom orssa-mentoo?*
Is there in this city a ... repair shop?	*Há nesta cidade alguma oficina de serviço oficial ...?*	*Are neshta see-darde algooma ofee-seena the servee-ssoo ofee-seaal ...?*
How long will it take to fix it?	*Quanto tempo durará a reparação?*	*Kwantoo tempo doo-rar-rar a repara-sowng?*
Please, check..., fix...	*Por favor, veri-fique..., repare...*	*Poor favor, veree-feeque..., repar...*
Could you change the spark plugs?	*Pode mudar as velas?*	*Pod moodar ash vel-ash?*
I have a puncture in my rear left tyre.	*Tenho um furo no pneu traseiro esquerdo.*	*Tay-gnoo oom fooroo noo pneoo traz-aeroo esh-kierdoo.*
The right light bulb is out.	*Fundiu-se a lâmpada do farol direito.*	*Foondee-oosse a lampada do farole dee-raytoo.*

2.4.6. Accidents

| Someone has had an accident at the mile marker..., ... quilometres from here. | *Deu-se um acidente ao quilómetro..., a... quilómetros daqui.* | *Deoo-sse oom assee-dente ow kilo-metro..., a ...kilo-metroosh d'key.* |
| There is someone badly hurt, slightly hurt. | *Há feridos graves, ligeiros.* | *Are free-doosh grar-vesh, lee-jayroosh.* |

Please, call the police.	*Por favor, chame a polícia.*	*Poor favor shame a poleecia.*
Where is the nearest hospital?	*Onde fica o hospital mais próximo?*	*Ond fee-ca oo hosh-peetal mysh pro-ssemo?*
Call a doctor!	*Chamem um médico!*	*Shamain oom medicoo!*
Call an ambulance right away.	*Chamem depressa uma ambulância!*	*Shamain depressa ooma am-boolancia!*
Are you hurt?	*Você está ferido?*	*Vos-sear eshtar fe-reedoo?*
Please, don't move!	*Não se mexa, por favor.*	*Now sse mersha, poor favor.*
My insurance company is..., here is my policy...	*A minha companhia de seguros é..., aqui está a minha apólice.*	*A mee-gna compania the segooroosh air..., Akey eshtar a mee-gna apo-lease.*
Have you been a witness to the accident?	*Você foi testemunha do ocorrido?*	*Vos-sear foi tesh-temoogna do occo-reedoo?*
Could you give me your name and address to find you if I need to?	*Pode dar-me o seu nome e morada para que possamos localizá-lo em caso de necessidade?*	*Pod dar-mer o seoo nome ee moorada para ker poss-amosh localee-zar-loo ayng cazoo the nesse-seedarde?*
Did you see the number plate of the car that didn't stop?	*Viu a matrícula do veículo que não parou?*	*Vee-oo a matree-coola do ve-eecoo-loo ker nowng parou?*

Vocabulary

accelerator	*acelerador*	*ass-larador*
accident	*acidente*	*asee-dente*
antifreeze	*anticongelante*	*anti-congelant*
battery	*bateria*	*batter-rear*
bulb	*lâmpada*	*lampada*
carburettor	*carburador*	*car-boorador*
chassis	*chassis*	*chassis*
clutch	*embraiagem*	*embrearjane*
crossing	*cruzamento*	*cruiser-mento*
curve	*curva*	*coorva*
distilled water	*água destilada*	*are-gua desh-teelada*
driver	*condutor*	*con-dootour*
exhaust pipe	*tubo de escape*	*tooboo the esh-carpe*
filter	*filtro*	*filtroo.*
frame	*carroçaria*	*caross-arear*
keys	*chaves*	*shavesh*
radiator	*radiador*	*radeeador*
rear-view mirror	*espelho retrovisor*	*esh-paylhoo retro-veesor*
screw	*parafuso*	*para-foozoo*

seatbelt	*cinto de segurança*	*seen-too the se-gooran-ssa*
shock	*amortecedor*	*a-mort-ssedor*
spare part	*peça sobresselente*	*pairssa sobsselente*
spark plug	*vela*	*velar*
starter	*ignição*	*eegneesowng*
steering wheel	*volante*	*volante*
trunk	*capô*	*car-po*
tyre	*pneu*	*pneoo*

2.5. Train and train station

Could you tell me where the train station is?	*Pode dizer-me onde fica a estação de caminhos-de-ferro?*	*Pod deezer-mer ond fee-ca a eshta-sowng the car-mee-gnoosh the fairroo?*
When does the train leave for...?	*A que horas sai o comboio para...?*	*A ker orash sy o comboyo para...?*
Does the train goes directly to...?	*O comboio é directo para...?*	*Oo comboyo air deeretoo para....?*
What platform does it leave from?	*De que linha, plataforma, parte?*	*The ker lee-gna, plataforma, part?*
Give me a ticket for... first class, second class.	*Dê-me um bilhete para..., de primeira, de segunda classe.*	*Dear mer oom bee-llet para..., the pree-mayra, se-goonda class.*

How much is the ticket to...?	*Quanto custa o bilhete para...?*	*Kwanto cooshta oo bee-llet para...?*
And a round trip ticket?	*E um bilhete de ida e volta?*	*Ee oom bee-llet the eeda ee volta?*
Are there coupons for ten, twenty trips?	*Têm conjuntos de módulos de dez, vinte viagens?*	*Tayng con-joontoosh the desh vingte viarjanes?*
How long will the train stop here?	*O comboio pára aqui durante quanto tempo?*	*Oo comboyo para akey do-rant kwantoo tempoo?*
I would like to check in my luggage.	*Queria registar as minhas malas.*	*Kria regeeshtar ash mingash marlash.*

Vocabulary

bed car	*carruagem-cama*	*Carrooajane-Cama*
bunk	*beliche*	*Beleashe*
car	*carruagem*	*Carrooajane*
compartment	*compartimento*	*Comparteementoo*
corridor	*corredor*	*Coorredor*
left luggage-office	*depósito de bagagem*	*Depozeetoo the bagajane*
line	*linha*	*Lee-gna*
locomotive	*locomotiva*	*Locomoteeva*

machinist	*maquinista*	*Makeeneeshta*
passenger	*passageiro*	*Passajayroo*
platform	*plataforma*	*Plataforma*
reservation	*reserva*	*Resairva*
schedule	*horário*	*Orário*
ticket	*bilhete*	*Beellet*
ticket reviewer	*revisor*	*Reveesor*
train station manager	*chefe de estação*	*Chef the eshtasowng*
waiting room	*sala de espera*	*Sala the eshpera*
window	*janela*	*Janela*

2.6. Airplane and the airport

How long does it take to get from the hotel to the airport?	*Quanto tempo se demora do hotel ao aeroporto?*	*Kwantoo tempo ser demora do otel ow airoportoo?*
How early should I be at the airport?	*Com que antecedência devo estar no aeroporto?*	*Com ker antserdencia dervoo eshtar noo airoportoo?*
I want a first class ticket, an economy ticket, for the flight to...	*Quero um bilhete de primeira classe, de classe turística, no voo para...*	*Keroo omm beellet the preemayra class, the class toureesteeca, noo voor para...*

I would like to change the date of departure, of return.	*Gostaria de alterar a data da partida, de regresso.*	*Goshtarear the alterar a data the parteeda, the regressoo.*
I would like to confirm my reservation.	*Queria confirmar o bilhete.*	*Kria con-feermar o beellet.*
Where is the desk to check in the luggage? The airline company is...	*Onde fica o balcão para efectuar o check-in da bagagem? A companhia aérea é a...*	*Ond fee-ca o balcowng para efetooar oo check-in da bagajane? A compagneea area air a...*
How much is the ticket?	*Quanto custa o bilhete?*	*Kwantoo coosta oo beellet?*
What is maximum luggage weight allowed?	*Qual é o limite de peso admitido sem sobretaxa?*	*Kual air oo limit the pezoo admeeteedoo sain sobretasha?*
At what time does the flight leave?	*A que horas sai o voo?*	*A ker orash sy o voor?*
Is there a waiting room?	*Existe uma sala de espera?*	*Ezeeshte ooma sala de eshpera?*
Where is the boarding gate?	*Onde fica a porta de embarque?*	*Ond fee-ca a porta the embark?*
When do we go aboard?	*A que horas embarcaremos?*	*A ker orash em barcamosh?*
I would like a smoking seat, non smoking seat.	*Queria um lugar de fumador, não fumador.*	*Kria oom loogar the foomador, nowng foomador.*

I only have hand luggage.	*Levo apenas bagagem de mão.*	*Lev apenash bagajane the mowng.*
I'm missing a suitcase, where can I file a claim?	*Falta-me uma mala, onde posso reclamá-la?*	*Falta-mer ooma mala, ond possoo reclamar-la?*
Here is your boarding pass with all the flight details.	*Aqui tem o seu cartão de embarque com todos os pormenores de voo.*	*Akey tain o seoo cartaoo the embark com todosh oosh proomenoresh the voor.*
Those suitcases need to be checked in.	*Essas malas têm de passar pelo check-in.*	*Essash malash tain ker passar pelo check-in.*
The plane will make a stop-over in...	*O avião fará escala em...*	*Oo avee-owng fara eshcala ayng...*
When we arrive at the airport where we will stop-over, go to the office of the airline.	*À chegada ao aeroporto de escala, apresente-se aos balcões da sua companhia.*	*Ah-shegarda ow airriportoo the eshcala, apresentesse ows balcoinsh da sewer compagnia.*
How long is the flight delayed for?	*Que atraso tem o voo?*	*Ker atrarzoo tain o voor?*
The flight is delayed for..., it has been canceled due to the fog.	*O voo está com um atraso de..., foi cancelado por causa do nevoeiro.*	*Ooo voor eshtar com omm atrarzoo the..., foy cancelardoo poor cowza do nevoo-ayroo.*

Please, take me to terminal number one, international, national.	*Por favor, leve-me ao terminal número 1, doméstico, internacional.*	*Poor favor, leve-mer ow termeenal noomeroo oomm doomaishteekoo, internacional.*

Vocabulary

airline company	*companhia aérea*	*com-par-gnee-a area*
airplane	*avião*	*aviaoo*
airport	*aeroporto*	*airoportoo*
airstrip	*pista*	*peeshta*
altitude	*altitude*	*altitude*
arrivals	*chegadas*	*shegardash*
boarding	*embarque*	*embark*
booth, cabin	*cabina*	*cabeena*
control of passports	*controlo de passaportes*	*controloo the passa-a- portesh*
control tower	*torre de controlo*	*torre the control*
domestic flight	*voo doméstico*	*voor doo-mais-tee-koo*
economy class	*classe económica*	*class eecoonomeeca*
emergency	*emergência*	*emergencia*
excess of baggage	*excesso de bagagem*	*acessoo the bagajane*

exit	*saída*	*saeeda*
first class	*primeira classe*	*preemayra class*
international flight	*voo internacional*	*voor internacional*
landing	*aterragem*	*aterrajane*
luggage	*bagagem*	*bagajane*
pilot	*piloto*	*peelotoo*
seat	*lugar*	*loogar*
seat belt	*cinto de segurança*	*seentoo the segooranssa*
stewardess	*hospedeira*	*oshpedayra*
stop-over	*escala*	*eshcala*
take off	*descolagem*	*deshcoolajane*
ticket	*bilhete*	*beelhet*
wing	*asa*	*aza*

2.7. Ships and the port

I would like a ticket to...	*Queria uma passagem para...*	*Kria ooma passajane para...*
What day does the ship sail to... and what is it called?	*Em que dia sai o barco para... e qual é o nome dele?*	*Ayng ker deer sy oo barcoo para... Ee kwal air oo nome deal?*
Is there a regular service?	*Há um serviço regular?*	*Are oom serveessoo regoolar?*

Give me a first class cabin, second class, cover...	*Dê-me um bilhete, camarote de primeira, segunda, coberta...*	*Dear-mer oom beelhet camarot the preemayra, segoonda, coberta...*
How long is the voyage?	*Quanto tempo dura a travessia?*	*Kwanto tempo doora a travessia?*
How many and what stops does it make?	*Quantas e que escalas faremos?*	*Kwantash ee ker eshcalash ferrearmosh?*
What is the port, the departing dock, boarding... of arrival?	*Qual é o porto, cais de saída, de embarque... de chegada?*	*Kwal air oo port, Kysh the saeeda, the embark... the shegada?*
I'm dizzy, sick, I need to see a doctor.	*Estou maldisposto, enjoado, preciso de um médico.*	*Eshtor maldeesh-poshtoo, enjoardoo, preseezoo the oom medico.*

Vocabulary

adrift	*deriva*	*dereeva*
boarding	*embarque*	*embark*
bow	*proa*	*proa*
cabin	*camarote*	*camerot*
captain	*capitão*	*capitaoo*
coast	*costa*	*coshta*

coast guard	guarda-costeira	gooarda coshtayra
cover	coberta	coberta
crew	tripulação	treepoolassao
cruise	cruzeiro	cruise-ayro
direction	rota	rota
dock, quay	cais	kysh
helm	leme	leme
island	ilha	ee-llea
life jacket	colete salva-vidas	coolet salva-veedash
lifeboat	bote salva-vidas	bot salva veedash
lighthouse	farol	farol
port	porto	portoo
sailing	navegação	navegasowng
sailor	marinheiro	maree-gnayroo
sea	mar	mar
ship doctor	médico de bordo	medicoo the bordoo
shipwreck	naufrágio	now-fragio
stern	popa	porper
to sail away	zarpar	zarpar
transatlantic	transatlântico	trans-atlanteecoo
voyage	travessia	travesseea
wave	onda	onda

3. City

3.1. Public transport

3.1.1. Taxi

Where can I get a taxi?	*Onde posso apanhar um táxi?*	*Ond poss apanghar oom táxi?*
Could you please get me a taxi?	*Pode chamar-me um táxi, por favor?*	*Pod shamar-mer oom táxi, poor favor?*
What is the additional fee for luggage, airport, station...?	*Qual é o suplemento para a bagagem, aeroporto, estação...?*	*Kwal air oo sooplementoo para a bagajane, airoportoo, a eshtasowng...?*
Please, take me to this address, to the airport, to the station.	*Leve-me a este endereço, ao aeroporto, à estação.*	*Leve-me a eshter endee-resoo, ow airoportoo, a eshtasowng.*
Please, stop here.	*Pare aqui, por favor.*	*Para akey, poor favor.*
Could you help me with my luggage?	*Poderia ajudar-me a levar a bagagem?*	*Pooderear ajoodar-mer a levar a bagajane?*
Could you wait for me?	*Pode esperar por mim?*	*Pod eshperar poor meeng?*
How much do I owe you?	*Quanto lhe devo?*	*Kwanto lle devoo?*

Could you give me a receipt?	*Pode passar-me um recibo?*	*Pod Passr-mer oom reseeboo?*

3.1.2. Bus

Where does the bus number... have a stop?	*Onde é a paragem do autocarro número...?*	*Ond air a parajane do autocarroo noomeroo...?*
How often does it come by?	*Passa com que frequência?*	*Passa com ker frekwencia?*
To go to... what bus should I take?	*Para ir até..., que autocarro devo apanhar?*	*Pra ear atair..., ker autocarrooo devoo apagnar?*
I am in a hurry.	*Tenho pressa.*	*Tayngno pressa.*
Where is the nearest stop?	*Onde fica a paragem mais próxima?*	*Ond fee-ca a parajane mysh proseema?*
Could you tell me if this bus stops near...?	*Pode dizer-me se este autocarro passa perto de...?*	*Pod deezear-mer ser eeshter autocarroo passa pertoo the...?*
Could you tell me when we get there?	*Pode avisar-me quando chegarmos?*	*Pod aveezar-mer kwandoo shegarmosh?*
When do they start running in the morning and when do they stop at night?	*Qual é a hora a que começam a circular de manhã e até que horas da noite?*	*Kwal air a ora a ker coomairsowng a circoolar demayngha ee atairker orash the noyt?*

3.1.3. Subway

Where is the nearest subway station?	*Onde fica a estação de metro mais próxima?*	*Ond fee-ca a eshtasowng the metro mysh proseema?*
When does the subway start, stop, running?	*A que horas abre, fecha, o metro?*	*A ker orash abre, faysha, o metro?*
How much is the ticket, the coupon?	*Qual é o preço do bilhete, do passe?*	*Kwal air oo priersso do beellet, doo pass?*
To go to..., what subway line should I take?	*Para ir até..., que linha de metro devo seguir?*	*Para eer atair..., ker lingna the metro devoo segere?*
In what station should I change trains?	*Em que estação devo fazer transbordo?*	*Ayng Ker eshtasowng devoo far-zeer transbordoo?*

3.2. Accomodation

3.2.1. Hotel

3.2.1.1. Reception

| I have a reservation in my name, in ...'s name. | *Reservei um quarto em meu nome, em nome de...* | *Rezervay oom kwartoo ayng meoo nome, ayng nome the...* |
| Good morning, good afternoon, good evening. Do you have any rooms left? | *Bom dia, boa tarde, boa noite. Tem quartos livres?* | *Bon dear, boa tard, boa noyt. Tayng kwartoosh leevresh?* |

Does the hotel have a garage?	O hotel tem garagem?	Oo otel tayng garajane?
So, where can I park the car?	Nesse caso, onde posso estacionar o carro?	Nesse cazoo, ond posso eshtaseeonar oo carroo?
I have the luggage in the trunk.	Tenho a bagagem na mala do carro.	Tay-gnoo a bagajane na marla do carroo.
Here are the keys, it's the room number...	Aqui tem as chaves, o quarto é o número...	Akey tayng ash shavesh, oo kwartoo air oo noomeroo...
I want a double room, a single room, with a bathroom, for... days.	Queria um quarto duplo, individual, com casa de banho, para... dias.	Kria oom kwartoo dooploo, indeveedual, con caza the bagnoo, para... diash.
Does the room have a telephone?	O quarto tem telefone?	Oo kwartoo tayng telefon?
How much is the room per day?	Qual é o preço por dia?	Kwal air o priersso poor dear?
Is breakfast included?	O pequeno-almoço está incluído?	Ooo peekiernoo almossoo eshtar inclooeedoo?
How much is full board, bed and breakfast?	Quanto custa a pensão completa, meia pensão?	Kwantoo cooshta a pensowng completa, maya pensowng?
Here is my identification card, my passport.	Aqui está o meu bilhete de identidade, passaporte.	Akey eshtar oo meoo beellet the eedenteedarde, passa-a-port.

When should I leave the room?	A que horas deverei deixar o quarto?	A ker orash deveray daysahar oo kwartoo?
Could you give me the key...?	Pode dar-me a chave...?	Pod dar-mer a shaver...?
Could you please get my bill ready?	Pode preparar-me a conta, por favor?	Pod preparar-mer a conta, poor favor?
Is there any mail for me, any phone messages?	Há correio para mim, alguma mensagem telefónica?	Are coray-oo para me, algooma mensajane telefoneeca?
Could you wake me up at...?	Pode acordar-me às... horas?	Pod acoordar-mer ash...orash?
I will leave tomorrow morning, afternoon, evening.	Partirei amanhã de manhã, à tarde, à noite.	Partee-ray amagnang de mangha, are tard, are noyt.
Could you tell me what this charge is for?	Pode explicar-me a que se refere esta parcela?	Pod eshpleecar-mer a ker ser refaire eshta parcela?
Don´t forget to return the keys when you leave the hotel.	Não se esqueça de entregar as chaves quando sair do hotel.	Now ser eshkessa the entregare ash shavesh kwando saeer do otel.
Do you have a storage to leave my luggage until I leave?	Têm algum local onde a bagagem possa ficar até eu partir?	Tayng algoom loocal ond a bagajane possa feecar ataïr eroo parteer?

Do you take credit cards?	Aceitam cartões de crédito?	Asaytaoo cartoins the credeetoo?
Could you send for my luggage?	Pode mandar alguém trazer a minha bagagem?	Pod mandar algain trazer a migna bagajane?
Could you get a taxi?	Pode chamar um táxi?	Pod shamar oom táxi?

3.2.1.2. Services

Am I speaking with the bar, restaurant, laundry room, reception?	Estou a falar para o serviço de bar, restaurante, lavandaria, recepção?	Eshtor a falar para oo serveessoo de bar, restaurante, lavandarear, recesowng?
I would like my pants / trousers, shirts, to be picked up to be washed, ironed.	Agradecia que recolhessem as calças, camisas, para lavar, passar a ferro.	Agradecia ker recoolhessen ash calssash, cameezash, para lavar, passar a fair-roo.
I would like my shoes to be cleaned.	Queria que me limpassem os sapatos.	Kria ker mer limpassen osh sapatoosh.
Does the hotel have a translating service?	O hotel dispõe de um serviço de intérprete?	O otel deeshpoing de oom serveessoo de interprete?
Could you bring me breakfast, a bottle of water, something to eat, to my room?	Por favor, traga-me ao quarto o pequeno-almoço, uma garrafa de água, qualquer coisa para comer.	Poor favor, traga-mer oow kwartoo o pequenoo almossoo, ooma garrafa de are-gua, kwal care coiza para coomer.

English	Portuguese	Pronunciation
At what time is breakfast, lunch, dinner served?	*A que horas se inicia o serviço de pequenos-almoços, almoços, jantares?*	*A ker orash ser eeneecia oo serveessoo de pequenosh almossoosh, almossoosh jantaresh?*
I would like you to bring me another blanket, bath towel.	*Gostaria que me trouxessem outro cobertor, um toalhão de banho.*	*Goshtarear ker mer troussessem outro cobertour oom twarlleeowng the bagno.*
The heating, air conditioning, television, hot water, doesn't work.	*O aquecimento, o ar condicionado, a televisão, a água quente, não funciona.*	*Oo akesseementoo o are condeesseeonado, a telezowng, a aregua kente, nowng fungseeona.*
Where is the bar, the hairdresser, the hall, the dining room?	*Onde é o bar, o cabeleireiro, a sala de estar, a sala de jantar?*	*Ond air oo bar, o cabelay-ray-roo, a sala the eshtar, a sala the jantar?*
I need paper, envelopes and stamps.	*Necessito de papel, envelopes e selos.*	*Nessesseetoo the papel, envelopesh ee sealosh.*
The room is not made up.	*O quarto não está arrumado.*	*Oo kwartoo now eshtar arroomado.*
Do you have postcards?	*Têm postais?*	*Tayng poshtiesh?*

City

Vocabulary

bathrobe	*roupão*	*roupowng*
bathtub	*banheira*	*ba-gnay-ra*
bed	*cama*	*cama*
comb	*pente*	*pente*
complaints	*reclamações*	*reclamassoinsh*
do not disturb	*não incomodar*	*nowng incomoodar*
elevator, lift	*elevador*	*eelevador*
emergency stairway	*escada de emergência*	*eshcada the emergenceea*
faucet	*torneira*	*tournayra*
fire exit	*saída de incêndio*	*saeeda de incendeeoo*
no vacancy	*completo*	*completoo*
porter	*recepcionista*	*ressecioneeshta*
razor	*máquina de barbear*	*markeena the barbeear*
slippers	*chinelos*	*sheenailoosh*
soap	*sabonete*	*saboonete*
tip	*gorjeta*	*gorjeta*
toothbrush	*escova de dentes*	*eshcova the dentesh*
toothpaste	*pasta dentífrica*	*pashta dentreefeeca*
towel	*toalha*	*twoalla*
waitress	*empregada*	*empregarda*

3.2.2. Apartments and private homes

I wish to rent an apartment, a private home, a country home.	*Queria alugar um apartamento, uma casa particular, uma casa de campo.*	*Kria aloogar oom apartamentoo, ooma caza parteecoolar, ooma caza the campo.*
I would like to rent it for... days, ... months.	*Queria fazer o aluguer por um período de... dias, ... meses.*	*Kria fazer oo aloogare por oom pereeoood the...dears,...merzesh.*
I will need two, three, rooms in the apartment.	*Preciso que o apartamento tenha dois, três, quartos.*	*Preseezoo ker oo apartamentoo tayngna doish, tresh, kwartoosh.*
Do I need to leave a deposit?	*É necessário deixar um sinal?*	*Air nessessario dayshar oom seenal?*
Is dinnerware, bed linen and bath linen included in the rent?	*No aluguer, está incluído o serviço de loiça, a roupa de cama e de banho?*	*No aloogare, eshtar inclooeedoo o serveessooo the loissa, a roupa the cama e the bagno?*
Does it have appliances?	*Tem electrodomésticos?*	*Tayng electrodoomesh-teecoosh?*
Is the water, light, heating included in the rent?	*No aluguer estão incluídos os consumos de água, luz e aquecimento?*	*No aloogare eshtaowng inclooeedosh osh conssoomoosh the are-gua, loosh e akeseementoo?*

Does the apartment have a pool? Is there a playground for children?	*O apartamento tem piscina? F. zona de recreio para as crianças?*	*Oo apartamentoo tayng peeshseena?Ee zona the recrayoo para as creeansash?*
I would like the apartment to be in a quiet area.	*Gostaria que o apartamento ficasse num local tranquilo.*	*Goshtarear ker oo apartamentoo feecasse noom loocal trankueelo.*
I would like the apartment to be oceanside.	*Gostaria de um apartamento que ficasse situado à beira-mar.*	*Goshtarear the oom apartamentoo que feecasse seetooador are bayra mar.*

Vocabulary

attic	*sótão*	*sawtown*
backyard	*pátio*	*pateeo*
basement	*cave*	*carve*
bathroom	*casa de banho*	*caza de bayngno*
bedroom	*quarto de dormir*	*kwartoo the doormeer*
ceiling	*tecto*	*tair-ctoo*
closet	*roupeiro*	*roupayroo*
contract	*contrato*	*contratoo*
corridor	*corredor*	*coorredor*
decoration	*decoração*	*decoorasowng*

dining room	*sala de jantar*	*sala the jantar*
dishes	*loiça*	*loissa*
dishwasher	*máquina de lavar loiça*	*markeena the lavar loissa*
door	*porta*	*porta*
floor	*piso*	*peezoo*
for rent	*aluga-se*	*alooguess*
furnished	*mobilado*	*moobeelado*
garage	*garagem*	*garajane*
garden	*jardim*	*jardeem*
ground floor	*rés-do-chão*	*resh doo shaowng*
heating	*aquecimento*	*akeseementoo*
house	*casa*	*caza*
kitchen	*cozinha*	*coo-zee-gna*
microwave	*microondas*	*meecro-ondash*
portal	*átrio*	*atreeo*
rent	*aluguer*	*aloogare*
roof	*telhado*	*ter-lla-doo*
room	*divisão*	*deveezaowng*
shower	*duche*	*doosh*
television set	*televisor*	*televeesor*
washer	*máquina de lavar roupa*	*markeena the lavar roupa*
window	*janela*	*janair-la*

3.2.3. Camping

Do you have a camping guide?	*Os senhores têm um guia de parques de campismo?*	*Osh senhyoresh tayng oom gere the parkesh the campeeshmoo?*
Is there a place to camp near here?	*Há algum parque de campismo próximo daqui?*	*Are algoom park the campeeshmoo proseemoo d'key?*
Can we camp here?	*Podemos acampar aqui?*	*Poodemosh acampar akey?*
How much is camping per day, per tent, per caravan, per car?	*Qual é o preço do acampamento por dia, por tenda, por caravana, por carro?*	*Kwal air o presso doo acampamnetoo poor dear, poor tender, poor caravana, poor carroo?*
Do you have sites with electric connections and drinkable water?	*Existem parcelas servidas de electricidade e de água potável?*	*Ezeeshten parcelash seveedash the electreeseedarde ee the are-gua pootarvel?*
Where are the showers, the restrooms, the toilets?	*Onde são os balneários, as casas de banho?*	*Ond sowng osh balneeareosh, ash cazash de bay-gno?*
Is there a supermarket near here?	*Há algum supermercado aqui perto?*	*Are algoom soopermercardoo akey pertoo?*

Vocabulary

bar	*cafetaria*	*cafetarear*
camping stove	*fogão portátil*	*foogaoo poortarteel*
can opener	*abre-latas*	*abre lartash*
canteen	*cantina*	*canteena*
corkscrew	*saca-rolhas*	*saca rolhash*
emergency kit	*caixa de primeiros socorros*	*kysha the preemayrosh socorrosh*
flashlight	*lanterna*	*lanterna*
fold out chair	*cadeira desdobrável*	*cadayra deshdoobravel*
gas tubes	*bilha de gás*	*beellea the gash*
guest house	*estalagem*	*eshtalajane*
layaway bed	*cama desdobrável*	*cama desdoobravel*
shelter	*refúgio*	*refoogeeoo*
sleeping bag	*saco-cama*	*sacoo cama*
tent	*tenda de campismo*	*tender the campishmoo*
thermos	*termo*	*termoo*

City

3.3. Food

3.3.1. Restaurant

Where can you eat well, cheap?	*Onde se pode comer bem, barato?*	*Ond se pod comer bain, barartoo?*
Could we take this table?	*Podemos ocupar esta mesa?*	*Poodemmosh ocoopar eshtar merza?*
We would like to make a reservation for a table for... and for... people.	*Queríamos reservar uma mesa para as... horas e para... pessoas.*	*Kremoosh reservar ooma merza para ash... orash ee para... pessoash.*
A table near the window, set apart, without much noise.	*Uma mesa junto à janela, isolada, sem muito barulho.*	*Ooma mearza joontoo are janair-la eezoolada sain mooito bahroollio.*
Without salt, sauce, lightly salted, well done, medium rare, medium.	*Sem sal, molho, pouco salgado, bem passado, mal passado, no ponto.*	*Sain sal, molloo, porkcoo salgardoo, bain passardoo.mal passardoo, noo pontoo.*
Waiter, please, an aperitif.	*Por favor, traga- -nos um vinho de aperitivo.*	*Poor favor, trarga- noosh oom vee-gnoo de aperreeteevoo.*
Waiter, serve us the special of the day.	*Por favor, desejávamos o prato do dia.*	*Poor favor dezejamoosh oo prartoo do dear.*
Let me have the menu, please.	*Traga-me a ementa, por favor.*	*Trarga-mer a eementa, poor favor.*

Please, bring us wine from this country, this area, house wine, water.	*Queremos vinho nacional, desta região, da casa, água.*	*Keremoosh vingnoo nacceonal, deshtar regeeaoo, da carza, are-gua.*
Do you have any vegetarian dishes?	*Têm pratos vegetarianos?*	*Tayng prartoosh vegetareeanoosh?*
I want something quick, we're in a hurry.	*Quero qualquer coisa rápida, estamos com pressa.*	*Kaeroo kwalker coiza rarpeeda, eshtamoosh con pressa.*
Could you recommend something to eat, something typical of this area?	*Aconselhe-nos algo que possamos comer, um prato típico desta região.*	*Aconsayllea-noosh algo ker poossamoosh comear, oom prartoo teepeecoo deshtar regeeowng.*
That is enough, thank you.	*Assim é suficiente, obrigado.*	*Assin air soofee-see-ent, obreegardoo.*
What kind of cheeses do you have?	*Que tipos de queijo têm?*	*Ker teepoo the kayjoo tayng?*
What is the house speciality?	*Qual é a especialidade da casa?*	*Kwal air a eshpesee-aleedad da carza?*
What wine would you suggest we order?	*Que vinho nos aconselha a tomar?*	*Ker vee-gnoo noosh aconserlha a tomar?*
I would like some more, please.	*Queria um pouco mais, por favor.*	*Kria oom poucoo mysh poor favor.*

| Without condiments, we'll add them. | *Sem ser temperado, nós mesmos temperaremos.* | *Sain sear temperardo, nosh meshmoosh temperamoosh.* |

3.3.1.1. At the table　　　　　　　　　　Vocabulary

ashtray	*cinzeiro*	*sinzayroo*
bottle	*garrafa*	*garrarfa*
coffeepot	*cafeteira*	*cafetayra*
corkscrew	*saca-rolhas*	*saca- rrorlhash*
cruet stand	*galheteiro*	*galhetayroo*
cup	*chávena*	*sharvnar*
flat plate	*prato raso*	*prartoo rarzo*
fork	*garfo*	*garfoo*
glass	*copo*	*coppoo*
knife	*faca*	*farker*
menu	*ementa*	*eementa*
napkin	*guardanapo*	*gwardanarpoo*
saltcellar	*saleiro*	*salayroo*
sauce boat	*molheira*	*moolhayra*
small spoon	*colher de chá*	*coollair de shah*
soup plate	*prato de sopa*	*prartoo the sopa*
spoon	*colher*	*coollair*
stemmed glass	*copo alto*	*coppoo altoo*
sugar bowl	*açucareiro*	*assocar-rayroo*

table	*mesa*	*mearza*
table cloth	*toalha de mesa*	*toarlha the mearza*
teapot	*bule*	*bull*
toothpicks	*palitos*	*paleetosh*
tray	*bandeja*	*bandayja*
tureen	*terrina*	*terreena*

bechamel	*béchamel*	*bechamel*
butter	*manteiga*	*mantayga*
cinnamon	*canela*	*canella*
cream	*nata*	*nata*
fennel	*funcho*	*foonchoo*
garlic	*alho*	*alleoo*
hot pepper	*malagueta*	*malaguerta*
laurel	*louro*	*louroo*
margarine	*margarina*	*margareena*
mayonnaise	*maionese*	*myornaise*
mustard	*mostarda*	*mooshtarda*
oil	*azeite*	*azayt*
oregano	*orégão*	*oraegon*
parsley	*salsa*	*salsa*
pepper	*pimenta*	*peementa*
saffron	*açafrão*	*assafrowng*

City

salt	*sal*	*sal*
sauce	*molho*	*molleeo*
vinegar	*vinagre*	*veenagre*

3.3.1.3. Flavours and quality — Vocabulary

acid	*ácido*	*areceedoo*
bitter	*amargo*	*amargoo*
cold	*frio*	*freeoo*
delicious	*delicioso*	*deleeseeorzoo*
flat	*insosso*	*insonssoo*
flavourful, tasty	*saboroso*	*saboororzo*
fresh	*fresco*	*freshcoo*
good	*bom*	*bon*
hard	*duro*	*dooroo*
heavy	*pesado*	*pezardoo*
hot	*picante*	*peecante*
hot	*quente*	*kiernt*
light	*leve*	*laive*
lukewarm	*morno*	*mornoo*
salted	*salgado*	*salgardoo*
soft	*suave*	*sooarve*
sweet	*doce*	*dorsse*
tender	*tenro*	*tenrroo*

boiled	*fervido*	*ferveedoo*
breaded	*envolto*	*envoltoo*
breaded	*panado*	*panardoo*
cooked	*cozido*	*coozeedoo*
fried	*frito*	*freetoo*
frosted	*congelado*	*congelardoo*
grill	*churrasco*	*shoorrashcoo*
grilled	*assado na grelha*	*assardoo na graylha*
grilled	*grelhado*	*grerlladoo*
just right, medium	*no ponto*	*noo pontoo*
medium rare	*mal passado*	*mal passardo*
raw	*cru*	*crew*
roast	*assado no forno*	*assardoo noo fornoo*
salted	*salgado*	*salgardoo*
smoked	*fumado*	*foomadoo*
stew	*estufado*	*eshtoofardoo*
stewed	*guisado*	*geezardoo*
stuffed	*recheado*	*rersheeardoo*
thick	*espesso*	*eshpessoo*
well done	*bem passado*	*bain passardoo*

City

3.3.2. Food

chips	*batatas fritas*	*batartash freetash*
cold cuts	*carnes frias*	*carnesh freeash*
dry fruit	*frutos secos*	*frootoosh secoosh*
ham	*fiambre*	*feeambre*
large sausage	*salsichão*	*salseeshowng*
olives	*azeitonas*	*azaytonash*
pates	*pâtés*	*patés*
potato salad	*salada russa*	*salarda roossa*
salads	*saladas*	*salardash*
salted crackers	*bolachas salgadas*	*boolashash salgardash*
side dish	*entradas*	*entrardash*
smoked ham	*presunto*	*presuntoo*
smoked pork sausage	*chouriço*	*shoreeessoo*
smoked pork sausage	*chouriço de sangue*	*shoreeessoo the sang*
smoked salmon	*salmão fumado*	*salmaoo foomardoo*

Soups	Sopas	soups
bean soup	*sopa de feijão*	*sopa de fayjowng*
chick-pea soup	*sopa de grão*	*sopa the growng*

chicken broth	*canja*	*canja*
consommé	consommé	*consommé*
fish soup	*sopa de peixe*	*sopa the paysh*
meat soup	*sopa de carne*	*sopa the carne*
tunnipleat soup	*sopa de nabiças*	*sopa the narbeesash*
vegetable soup	*sopa de legumes*	*sopa the legoomesh*

Pasta	*Massas*	*mah-sash*
canneloni	*canelones*	*canellonesh*
lasagne	*lasanha*	*lasagne*
macaroni	*macarrão*	*macarraoo*
ravioli	*raviolis*	*ravioli*
spaghetti	*esparguete*	*eshparguet*

Vegetables	*Legumes*	*Legoomesh*
artichoke	*alcachofra*	*alcashofra*
asparagus	*espargos*	*eshpargoosh*
beet	*beterraba*	*baterrarba*
broccoli	*brócolos*	*brocooloosh*
brussels sprouts	*couve-de-bruxelas*	*corv the brooshelash*
cabbage	*acelga*	*asselga*
cabbage	*couve*	*corv*
carrot	*cenoura*	*cenorra*

celery	*aipo*	*aipo*
cucumber	*pepino*	*pepeenoo*
eggplant	*beringela*	*berinjela*
endives	*endívias*	*endeeveeash*
escarole	*chicória*	*sheecorrea*
garlic	*alho*	*alleoo*
green beans	*feijão-verde*	*fay-jowng verde*
leek	*alho-francês*	*alleoo francesh*
lettuce	*alface*	*alfarce*
mushrooms	*cogumelos*	*coogoomeloosh*
onion	*cebola*	*cebola*
peas	*ervilhas*	*erveellash*
pepper	*pimento*	*peementoo*
potato	*batata*	*batarta*
pumpkin	*abóbora*	*aboboora*
radish	*rabanetes*	*rabanetesh*
spinach	*espinafres*	*eshpeenafresh*
tomatoes	*tomate*	*tomate*

Beans	*Leguminosas*	*legoomee-nohsash*
beans	*feijão*	*fayjowng*
chickpeas	*grão-de-bico*	*grawng the beecoo*
lentils	*lentilhas*	*lenteelleeash*

Eggs	*Ovos*	*ovoosh*
boiled eggs	*ovos quentes*	*ovoosh kerntesh*
fried	*estrelados*	*eshtrelardoosh*
hard	*cozidos*	*coozeedoosh*
omelette	*omeleta*	*omelet*
poached	*escalfados*	*eshcalfardoosh*
scrambled	*mexidos*	*mesheedoosh*

3.3.2.3. Second course — Vocabulary

Fish	*Peixes*	*Pay-shesh*
anchovy	*anchova*	*anshouva*
cod	*bacalhau*	*bacalhaoo*
fried	*fritos*	*freetoosh*
gilthead	*dourada*	*dohrrarda*
grilled	*grelhados*	*grerllardoosh*
grouper	*mero*	*mero*
herring	*arenque*	*arenker*
in sauce	*em molho*	*ayng morlho*
mackerel	*cavala*	*cavala*
marinated	*marinados*	*mareenardoosh*
rooster	*peixe-galo*	*paysh galo*
salmon	*salmão*	*salmowng*

Meat	Carne	Karn
bacon	*toucinho*	*torseegnoo*
beef	*vaca*	*varca*
kid	*cabrito*	*cabreetoo*
lamb	*borrego*	*boorregoo*
pork	*porco*	*poucoo*
veal	*vitela*	*veetela*

Roasts and stews	Assados e guisados	Ar-sar-doosh ee gee-sar-doosh
breaded fillet	*panado*	*panardoo*
choped meat	*carne picada*	*carne peecarda*
fillet	*escalope*	*eshcalop*
hamburger	*hambúrguer*	*hamboorger*
kidney	*rim*	*rim*
lambchop	*costeleta de borrego*	*coshteleta the boorregoo*
leg	*perna*	*perna*
leg of lamb	*perna de borrego*	*perna the boorregoo*
liver	*fígado*	*feegadoo*
loin	*lombo*	*lomboo*
meat stew	*guisado de carne*	*geezardoo the carne*

meatballs	*almôndegas*	*almondergash*
porkchop	*costeleta de porco*	*coosteleta the porkoo*
roasted	*assado*	*assardoo*
sirloin	*acém (bife)*	*assem (beef)*
steak	*bife*	*beef*
stew	*estufado*	*eshtoofardoo*
T-bone steak	*costeleta de vaca*	*costeleta the varca*
tongue	*língua*	*leen-gooa*

City

Cheeses	*Queijos*	*Kayjoosh*
blue	*azul*	*azool*
cheese-curds	*requeijão*	*rekayjowng*
cured cheese	*curado*	*coorardoo*
fresh cheese	*fresco*	*freshcoo*
from cow's milk	*de vaca*	*the varca*
from goat's milk	*de cabra*	*the carbra*
from sheep's milk	*de ovelha*	*the ovaylleia*
melted cheese	*fundido*	*foondeedo*
semicured	*meio-curado*	*mayo coorardoo*
tender	*mole*	*mol*

Dry fruits	Frutos secos	Froo-toosh-saircoosh
almonds	*amêndoas*	*amendoash*
chestnuts	*castanhas*	*cashtagnash*
hazel-nuts	*avelãs*	*avelansh*
nuts	*nozes*	*norzesh*
pine nuts	*pinhões*	*pignoesh*
pistachios	*pistácios*	*pistashios*
sunflower seeds	*sementes de girassol*	*sementesh the geerassol*

Fruits	Fruta	Froo-tah
apple	*maçã*	*massan*
apricot	*damasco*	*damashcoo*
avocado	*abacate*	*abacat*
banana	*banana*	*banana*
blackberry	*amora*	*amora*
cherry	*cereja*	*cerayja*
coconut	*coco*	*corco*
date	*tâmara*	*tamara*
fig	*figo*	*feegoo*
grape	*uva*	*oova*
grapefruit	*toranja*	*toranja*
kiwi	*quivi*	*keevee*
lemon	*limão*	*leemowng*

mandarin	*tangerina*	*tangerrena*
mango	*manga*	*manga*
melon	*melão*	*melowng*
orange	*laranja*	*laranja*
pear	*pêssego*	*pierssegoo*
peach	*pêra*	*pera*
pineapple	*ananás*	*ananash*
plum	*ameixa*	*ameysha*
quince	*marmelo*	*marmeloo*
raspberry	*framboesa*	*franbooerza*
strawberry	*morango*	*morangoo*
watermelon	*melancia*	*melanceea*

Sweets and desserts	*Doces e sobremesas*	*Doh-cesh e soobre-maie-sash*
cream	*creme*	*creme*
cream	*nata*	*nata*
custard	*flã*	*flan*
honey	*mel*	*mel*
ice cream	*gelado*	*jelardoo*
marmalade	*compota*	*compota*
pudding	*pudim*	*poohding*
tart	*tarte*	*tart*
yogurt	*iogurte*	*yogoort*

Pastries	Pastelaria	Pash-telareea
bonbon	*bombom*	*bombom*
cake	*bolo*	*boh-loo*
chocolate	*chocolate*	*chocolat*
cookies	*biscoitos*	*beescoitoosh*
crackers	*bolachas*	*boolashash*
meringue	*merengue*	*merengue*
puff pastry	*massa folhada*	*marssa foollada*

Bread	Pão	Powng
corn-bread	*broa*	*broa*
fresh bread	*fresco*	*freshcoo*
grated bread	*ralado*	*ralardoo*
quick bread	*de forma*	*the forma*
roll bread	*pãozinho*	*powng-zee-gnoo*
rye bread	*de centeio*	*the centayoo*
wheat bread	*de trigo*	*the treegoo*
whole bread	*integral*	*integral*
without salt	*sem sal*	*sayng sal*

3.3.3. Drinks — Vocabulary

Water	Água	Ar-gooa
bottled	*engarrafada*	*engarrafarda*
mineral	*mineral*	*mineral*
sparkling	*com gás*	*con gash*

tap	*da torneira*	*da tornayra*
tap, mineral	*sem gás*	*sayng gash*
tonic	*tónica*	*tonica*

Coffee	*Café*	*Kar-fair*
black	*simples*	*sinplesh*
decaffeinated	*descafeinado*	*deshcafaynardoo*
espresso	*expresso*	*expresso*
long	*cheio*	*shayoo*
short	*curto*	*coortoo*
with a little milk	*pingado*	*pingardoo*
with ice	*com gelo*	*con jelo*
with milk	*com leite*	*con layte*
with sugar	*com açúcar*	*con asoocar*
without sugar	*sem açúcar*	*sayng assoocar*

Tea	*Chá*	*Char*
with honey	*com mel*	*com mel*
with lemon	*com limão*	*com leemowng*
with milk	*com leite*	*com layt*
with toast and butter	*com torradas e manteiga*	*com toorradash ee mantayga*

Beer	*Cerveja*	*Serwayjar*
black	*preta*	*preta*
lager	*branca*	*branca*

City

Wine	Vinho	Vinghoo
cold	fresco	freshcoo
dry	seco	secoo
red	tinto	tintoo
room temperature	natural	natooral
rose	rosé	rose
sweet	doce	dorss
white wine	branco	brancoo

Juices	Sumos	Soomoosh
lemonade	limonada	leemonarda
orange	de laranja	the laranja
tomato	de tomate	the tomate

Other drinks	Outras bebidas	Outrash bebeedash
anisette	anis	aneesh
brandy	aguardente	are-gua ardente
chocolate	chocolate	chocoolat
gin	gin	gin
infusions	infusões	infoozoesh
liquor	licor	leecor
milk	leite	layt
rum	rum	room
soda	soda	soda

3.3.4. Café and bar

Waiter, may I have a coffee with milk, please?	*Por favor, um café com leite.*	*poor favor, oom café con layt*
What will you have to drink?	*O que vão tomar?*	*oo ker vouwng toomar?*
I will have a..., Serve me a...	*Vou tomar... Sirva-me...*	*vor toomar... seerva-mer...*
Give me a little more...	*Traga-me um pouco mais de...*	*trarga-me oom poucoo mysh the..*
Will you please bring me the menu?	*Pode trazer-me a ementa, por favor?*	*pod trazer-mer a eementa, poor favor?*
Where is the public phone?	*Onde é o telefone público?*	*ond air oo telefone poobleecoo?*
Where are the toilets?	*Onde são as casas de banho?*	*ond sowng ash carzash the bay-gnoo?*
How much do I owe you?	*Quanto lhe devo?*	*kwanto lher dervoo?*

Vocabulary

appetizer	*aperitivo*	*apereeteevoo*
bar	*bar*	*bar*
beer	*cerveja*	*cervayja*
coffeepot	*cafeteira*	*cafetayra*

counter	*balcão*	*balcowng*
draft beer	*imperial*	*impereeal*
gin	*gin*	*gin*
ice	*gelo*	*jelo*
juice	*sumo*	*sumoo*
liquor	*licor*	*licoor*
soft drink	*refresco*	*refreshcoo*
tray	*bandeja*	*bandayja*

3.4. Shopping

3.4.1. Gifts and handicrafts

I would like to see if I can find something I like to take as a souvenir.	*Procuro qualquer coisa de que goste, para levar como recordação.*	*Procooro kwalcare coiza the ker goshtoo, pra levar comoo recoordasowng.*
I would like to buy crafts.	*Gostaria de comprar um objecto de artesanato.*	*Goshtaria the comprar oom objectoo the artezanartoo.*
What is the price of this statue, painting, craft...?	*Qual é o preço desta escultura, pintura, peça de artesanato...?*	*Kwal air oo prierssoo deshta eshcooltoora, pintoora, pairssa the artezanartoo...?*
Is this ceramic typical from this area?	*Esta cerâmica é típica da região?*	*Eshta cerameeca air teepeeca da regeeowng?*

| What crafts are typical from this area? | Que peças de artesanato são típicas desta região? | Ker pairssas the artezarnato sowng teepeecash deshta regee-owng? |
| Let me have these post cards. | Dê-me estes postais ilustrados. | Dearme eshtesh poshtaeesh eeloostradoosh. |

Vocabulary

ashtray	cinzeiro	sinzayroo
belt	cinto	seentoo
ceramic	cerâmica	cerameeca
cigarette case	cigarreira	seegarrayra
crystal	cristal	creeshtal
doll	boneca	boonairca
embroidery	bordado	boordardoo
handkerchief	lenço	lensoo
key ring	porta-chaves	porta sharvesh
lace	rendas	rendash
porcelain	porcelana	poorcelana
portfolio	pasta	pashta
table cloth	toalha de mesa	toalha the mairza
tie	gravata	gravata
toy	brinquedo	brinkierdoo
tray	bandeja	bandayja
umbrella	guarda-chuva	guarda shoova
vase	jarra	jar-rra
wallet	carteira	cartayra

3.4.2. Shops

Where is the shopping center, the supermarket, the shop...?	*Onde fica o centro comercial, o supermercado, a loja...?*	*Ond feeca oo centro coomercial, oo super mercado a loja...?*
How can I get there?	*Como posso ir até lá?*	*Commoo possoo eer atair la?*
Are there any department stores around here?	*Há alguns grandes armazéns aqui perto?*	*Are algooms grandesh armazensh akey pairtoo?*
Good morning, good afternoon, I would like to buy...	*Bom dia, boa tarde, queria comprar...*	*Bon dear, boa tard, kria comprar...*
I would like to try it on.	*Gostaria de experimentar.*	*Goshtaria the eshpereementar.*
Could you show me something else?	*Pode mostrar-me outras peças?*	*Pod mooshtrar-me outrash pairsash?*
How much is it?	*Quanto custa?*	*Kwantoo cooshta?*
Do you have anything less expensive?	*Não tem nada mais em conta?*	*Nowng tayng nada maeesh en conta?*
I don't like it. I like it very much, but it's too expensive.	*Não gosto. Gosto muito, mas é muito caro.*	*Nao goshtoo. Goshtoo moitoo, mash air moitoo caro.*
I'll take it. Do you accept credit cards?	*Vou levá-lo. Aceitam cartões de crédito?*	*Vou levar-loo. Asaytam cartoesh the crairdeetoo?*

| I would like to exchange this article of clothing, this thing. Here is the receipt. | *Gostaria de trocar esta peça de roupa, este objecto. Aqui está o recibo.* | *Goshtaria the troocar eshta pairssa the roupa, eshte objectoo. Akey eshtar oo receeboo.* |
| Where can I find an umbrella? | *Onde posso encontrar um guarda-chuva?* | *Ond possoo encontrar oom guarda-shoova?* |

Vocabulary

antiques	*antiguidades*	*antygueedadesh*
carpets	*tapetes*	*tapetesh*
clerk	*empregado*	*empregardoo*
clothes	*roupa*	*roupa*
disk	*disco*	*deeshcoo*
fabrics	*tecidos*	*teseedoosh*
furniture	*móvel*	*movel*
gifts	*prendas*	*prendash*
housewares	*artigos domésticos*	*arteegoosh doomairsh-teecoosh*
newspaper	*jornal*	*joornal*
salesman	*vendedor*	*vendedor*
schedule	*horário*	*orario*
shoes	*sapatos*	*sapatoosh*
to buy	*comprar*	*comprar*
to choose	*escolher*	*esh-coo-llear*
to exchange	*trocar*	*troocar*

City

to return	*devolver*	*devolver*
to spend	*gastar*	*gashtar*
to try on	*experimentar*	*eshpereementar*
toys	*brinquedos*	*brinkierdoosh*
watch	*relógio*	*relogio*
window	*montra*	*montra*

3.4.2.1. Florist

I would like a bouquet	*Queria um ramo de flores...*	*Kria oom ramoo the floresh...*
How are these flowers called?	*Como se chamam estas flores?*	*Commoo ser shamam eshtash floresh?*
I would like this centerpiece, this pot of...	*Queria este centro, arranjo de...*	*Kria eshte centroo, arranjoo the...*
Can you send these flowers to this address?	*Pode enviar este ramo de flores a este endereço?*	*Pod enveear eshte ramoo the floresh a eshte enderessoo?*
Send it this afternoon, tomorrow morning.	*Envie-o esta tarde, amanhã de manhã.*	*Enveeo eshta tard, ama-gnang the ma-gnang.*

Vocabulary

azalea	*azálea*	*azaleea*
bouquet	*ramo*	*ramoo*
camellia	*camélia*	*camairleea*

carnation	*cravo*	*cravoo*
chrysanthemum	*crisântemo*	*creezanshtemoo*
dahlia	*dália*	*daleea*
daisy	*margarida*	*margareeda*
florist	*florista*	*floreeshta*
flower	*flor*	*flor*
flower shop	*florista (loja)*	*floreeshta (loja)*
gardenias	*gardénias*	*gardairneeash*
geranium	*gerânio*	*jeraneeo*
hyacinth	*jacinto*	*jaseentoo*
hydrangea	*hortênsia*	*ortenseea*
jasmine	*jasmin*	*jashmin*
leaf	*folha*	*folla*
lilac	*lilás*	*leelash*
lily	*lírio*	*leereeoo*
magnolia	*magnólia*	*magnoleea*
narcissus	*narciso*	*narseezoo*
orchid	*orquídea*	*orkeydeea*
plant	*planta*	*planta*
pot	*vaso*	*varzoo*
rose	*rosa*	*rosa*
tulip	*tulipa*	*tooleepa*
violet	*violeta*	*veeooleta*
white lily	*açucena*	*assoocena*

3.4.2.2. Photography

I would like this film developed matte, glossy. When will it be ready?	*Queria revelar este rolo em papel mate, em papel brilhante. Quando estará pronto?*	*Kria revelar eshte rolo ayng papel mate,ayng papel breelhante. Kwandoo eshtarar prontoo?*
I would like some copies made of these pictures and an anlargement of this other one.	*Queria fazer cópias destas fotografias e ampliar esta.*	*Kria fazer copeeash destash fotoografeeash ee ampleear eshta.*
I would like to have some passport pictures taken.	*Pretendia tirar algumas fotografias tipo passe.*	*Prentendear teerar algoomash fotoografeeash teepoo pass.*
Give me a colour film, brand name..., of twenty-four/ /thirty-six pictures.	*Dê-me um rolo a cores, marca..., de 24/36 fotografias.*	*Dearme oom roloo a coresh, marca..., the 24/36 fotoografeeash.*

Vocabulary

battery	*pilha*	*peelleea*
camera	*câmara*	*camera*
copy	*cópia*	*copeea*
development	*revelação*	*revelasowng*
diaphragm	*diafragma*	*deeafragma*

enlargement	*ampliação*	*ampleeasowng*
exhibition	*exposição*	*eshpoozeessowng*
film	*película*	*peleecoola*
filter	*filtro*	*feeltroo*
finder	*visor*	*veezor*
flash	*flash*	*flash*
glossy finish	*com brilho*	*con breelhoo*
matte	*mate*	*mate*
negative	*negativo*	*negateevoo*
objective	*objectiva*	*objecteeva*
picture	*fotografia*	*fotografeea*
positive	*positivo*	*poozeeteevoo*
projector	*projector*	*proojector*
size	*tamanho*	*tamanhoo*
slide	*diapositivo*	*deshpoozeeteevoo*
spool	*rolo*	*rolo*
test	*prova*	*prova*
to develop	*revelar*	*revelar*
trigger	*disparador*	*deshparador*
tripod	*tripé*	*treepair*
wide lens	*grande-angular*	*grand angoolar*
zoom lens	*teleobjectiva*	*telaobjecteeva*

3.4.2.3. Jewellery store and watchmaker's shop

English	Portuguese	Pronunciation
My watch gets behind, ahead. Could you check it?	*O meu relógio atrasa-se, adianta-se. Poderia consertar-mo?*	*Oo meoo relogioo atrarzasse, adeeantasse. Pooderia consertar-mo?*
How much will it cost to fix it?	*Em quanto ficará o arranjo?*	*Ayng kwantoo feecarar oo aranjoo?*
Could you change the wrisband of the watch?	*Poderia trocar a correia do relógio?*	*Pooderia troocar a cooraya doo relogio?*
I would like a gold chain. How many karats is it?	*Desejava um fio de ouro. Quantos quilates tem?*	*Dezejava oom feeo the oro. Kwantoosh keylatesh tayng?*
Could I take a look at this necklace, watch, earrings, rings...?	*Poderia ver esse colar, relógio, brincos, anel...?*	*Pooderia ver esse coolar, relogio, brincoosh, anel...?*

Vocabulary

English	Portuguese	Pronunciation
alarm clock	*despertador*	*deshpertador*
amber	*âmbar*	*ambar*
aquamarine	*água-marinha*	*argua – mareegna*
bracelet	*pulseira*	*pulsayra*
brilliant	*brilhantes*	*breelhantesh*
broch	*broche*	*brorshe*
chain	*fio*	*fee-oo*
choral	*coral*	*cooral*

chrome	*cromado*	*cromardoo*
chronometer	*cronómetro*	*cronormetro*
cross	*cruz*	*croosh*
diamond	*diamante*	*deeamante*
earrings	*brincos*	*brincoosh*
emerald	*esmeralda*	*eshmeralda*
gilding	*dourado*	*dourardoo*
gold	*ouro*	*oro*
hand	*ponteiro*	*pontayroo*
imitation jewellery	*bijuteria*	*beejooteeria*
ivory	*marfim*	*marfin*
jetty	*mola*	*mola*
jewel	*jóia*	*joya*
jeweller	*joalheiro*	*joalhayroo*
karats	*quilates*	*keelatesh*
lighter	*isqueiro*	*eeshkayroo*
locket	*medalhão*	*medalleowng*
minute hand	*ponteiro* *dos minutos*	*pontayroo doosh* *meenutoosh*
mount	*armação*	*armasowng*
necklace	*colar*	*coolar*
pearl	*pérola*	*pairola*
pin	*alfinete*	*alfeenete*
precious	*pedra preciosa*	*pedra preseeorza*
ring	*anel*	*anel*

ruby	*rubi*	*rubee*
sapphire	*safira*	*safeera*
second hand	*ponteiro dos segundos*	*pontayroo doosh segundoosh*
silver	*prata*	*prata*
stainless steel	*aço inoxidável*	*assoo-eenox-eedavel*
strap	*correia*	*coorraya*
turquoise	*turquesa*	*turkerza*
watch	*relógio*	*relogio*
wrist-stud	*botões de punho*	*botoesh the poognoo*

3.4.2.4. Bookshop, stationer's and kiosk

I would like a roadmap of...	*Queria um mapa de estradas de...*	*Kria oom mapa the eshtradsh the...*
I would like a city map. Do you have any books on the city?	*Queria um mapa da cidade. Tem algum livro sobre a cidade?*	*Kria oom mapa da seedard. Taygn algoom leevroo sobre a seedard?*
Do you have a bilingual guide book in... and...?	*Tem algum guia turístico bilingue, em... e...?*	*Tayng algoom geer toureesh-teecoo beelingoo, Ayng... Ee...?*
I would like a note book with graph paper.	*Queria um caderno quadriculado.*	*Kria oom cadernoo kadreecooladoo*
Do you have gift wrap?	*Tem papel para embrulhar presentes?*	*Tayng papel para embroolleear presentesh?*

I would like some stationery, envelops and postcards of the city.	*Queria papel de carta, envelopes e postais da cidade.*	*Kria papel the carta, envelopesh ee pooshteesh da seedad.*
Do you have any newspapers in... language?	*Tem jornais em língua...?*	*Tayng joornaeesh ayng língua...?*
How much is this comic?	*Quanto custa esta banda desenhada?*	*Kwantoo cooshta eshta banda dezegnarda?*
I would like the last issue of... magazine.	*Queria o último número da revista...*	*Kria oo ulteemoo noomeroo da reveeshta...*

Vocabulary

Bookshop	*Livraria*	*Leevraria*
anthology	*antologia*	*antooloogia*
atlas	*atlas*	*atlas*
author	*autor*	*autor*
biography	*biografia*	*beeografeea*
book	*livro*	*leevroo*
bookseller	*livreiro*	*leevrayroo*
catalogue	*catálogo*	*cataloogoo*
city map	*mapa da cidade*	*mapa da seedard*
collection	*colecção*	*coolairsowng*
comedy	*comédia*	*coomairdeea*

contents	*índice*	*indeece*
cover	*capa*	*capa*
dictionary	*dicionário*	*deeseeonario*
edition	*edição*	*edeesowng*
editorial	*editorial*	*edeetoorial*
encyclopedia	*enciclopédia*	*enseecloopairdeea*
essay	*ensaio*	*ensyeeoo*
grammar	*gramática*	*gramarteeca*
library	*estante*	*eshtante*
manual	*manual*	*manual*
memories	*memórias*	*memorriash*
novel	*romance*	*roomance*
poem	*poema*	*pooema*
poetry	*poesia*	*poeezeea*
publication	*publicação*	*poobleecasowng*
road map	*mapa de estradas*	*mapa the eshtrardash*
science	*ciência*	*seeencia*
science-fiction	*ficção científica*	*feexowng seenteefeeca*
short story	*conto*	*contoo*
title	*título*	*teetooloo*
tourist guide	*guia turístico*	*gia tooreeshteecoo*
translator	*tradutor*	*tradootor*
volume	*volume*	*vooloome*
work	*obra*	*obra*
writer	*escritor*	*eshcreetor*

Stationer's	Papelaria	Paplareea
ballpoint	esferográfica	eshfairograrfeeca
binder	pasta	pashta
bristol board	cartolina	cartooleena
calendar	agenda	agenda
calendar	calendário	calendario
cardboard	cartão	cart-owng
cards	baralho de cartas	barahlleoo the cartash
compass	compasso	comparssoo
envelope	envelope	envelope
eraser	borracha	boorarsha
fountain pen	caneta de tinta permanente	caneta the tinta permanente
glue	cola	cola
ink	tinta	tinta
label	etiqueta	eteekerta
marker	marcador	marcador
note pad	bloco de notas	blocoo the nortash
notebook	caderno	cadairnoo
paintbrush	pincel	peen-cel
paper	papel	pah-pail
pencil	lápis	lapeesh
photo album	álbum fotográfico	alboom footoografeecoo

City

How much do I owe you?	*Quanto lhe devo?*	*Kwantoo lher devoo?*
I need a shampoo for oily hair, dry, normal.	*Dê-me um champô para cabelos oleosos, secos, normais.*	*Dearme oom shampoh para cabeloosh oleeozoosh, secoosh, normaeesh.*
I would like a lotion and shaving cream.	*Queria um creme hidratante e um depilatório.*	*Kria oom creme eedratante ee oom depeelatorio.*
Could you give me... perfume?	*Queria um frasco de perfume, da marca...*	*Kria oom frashcoo the perfoomer, da marca...*
I would like a deodorant.	*Queria um desodorizante.*	*Kria oom dezordoorizant.*

Vocabulary

Hairdresser's	*Cabeleireiro*	*Kabelayrayroo*
bang	*franja*	*franja*
barber	*barbeiro*	*barbayroo*
beard	*barba*	*barba*
braid	*trança*	*transsa*
brush	*escova*	*eshcova*
brush	*pincel de barba*	*pincel the barba*
colored	*pintado*	*pintadoo*
colour	*cor*	*core*
cream	*creme*	*crème*
comb	*pente*	*pente*

curls	*caracóis*	*caracoeesh*
curls	*rolos*	*roloosh*
cut	*corte*	*corte*
dandruff	*caspa*	*cashpa*
dry	*seco*	*secoo*
dryer	*secador*	*secador*
friction	*fricção*	*freex-sowng*
hair	*cabelo*	*cabeloo*
hair spray	*laca*	*laca*
hairdresser	*cabeleireiro*	*cabelayrayroo*
hairline	*risco*	*reeshcoo*
hairstyle	*penteado*	*penteeadoo*
knife	*navalha*	*navalha*
lotion	*loção*	*loosowng*
manicure	*manicura*	*maneecoora*
mirror	*espelho*	*esh-pair-lleo*
mustache	*bigode*	*beegod*
nailpolish	*verniz*	*verneesh*
scissors	*tesoura*	*tezoura*
shampoo	*champô*	*shanpoh*
shaving	*barbear*	*barbeear*
sideburns	*patilhas*	*pateelleeash*
soap	*sabonete*	*saboonete*
tint	*tinta*	*tinta*
towel	*toalha*	*toalla*
wash	*lavagem*	*lavajane*
wavy	*ondulado*	*ondooladoo*
wig	*peruca*	*perooca*

City

Perfume shop	*Perfumaria*	*Per-foo-ma-reea*
baby powder	*pó de talco*	*po the talcoo*
cleansing milk	*leite de limpeza*	*layte the limpeza*
cologne	*água-de-colónia*	*argua the coloneea*
compresses	*compressas*	*compressash*
creams	*cremes*	*cremesh*
deodorant	*desodorizante*	*dezodooreezantesh*
eyeshadow	*sombra*	*sombra*
fingernail clipper	*corta-unhas*	*corta unhash*
knife	*navalha*	*navalha*
lipstick	*batom*	*baton*
make-up	*cosméticos*	*coshmairteecoosh*
make-up	*maquilhagem*	*makeylhajane*
mascara	*rímel*	*reemel*
nail polish remover	*acetona*	*assetona*
perfume	*perfume*	*perfoome*
shaving blade	*lâmina de barbear*	*lameena the barbeear*
sponge	*esponja*	*eshponja*
suntan oil	*óleo bronzeador*	*oleeo bronzeeador*
tissue	*lenços*	*lenssoosh*
toothbrush	*escova de dentes*	*eshcova the dentesh*
toothpaste	*pasta dentrífica*	*pashta dentreefeeca*
vaporizer	*vaporizador*	*vaporeezador*

3.4.2.6. Tobacco shop

I would like a packet of cigarettes, tobacco for pipe.	*Queria um maço de cigarros, tabaco para cachimbo.*	*Kria oom massoo the seegarrooshs, tabacoo para cashinboo*
Give me a box of matches, cigars.	*Dê-me uma caixa de fósforos, de charutos.*	*Dearme ooma Kyeesha the foshfooroosh, the sharootoosh.*
I would like a lighter.	*Queria um isqueiro.*	*Kria oom eshkayroo.*
Do you have pipe tobacco?	*Têm tabaco para cachimbo?*	*Tayng tabacoo para cashinboo?*
Could you fill up this lighter with fluid?	*Poderia carregar este isqueiro de gás?*	*Poodereea carregar eshte eshkayroo the gash?*

Vocabulary

cigar	*charuto*	*sharootoo*
cigarette box	*caixa de cigarros*	*kyeesha the seegarroosh*
cigarette-case	*cigarreira*	*seegarayra*
cigarette paper	*mortalha*	*moortahllea*
cigarettes	*cigarros*	*seegarroosh*
gas	*gás*	*gash*
gasoline	*gasolina*	*gazooleena*
lighter	*isqueiro*	*eshkayroo*
matches	*fósforos*	*foshfooroosh*

mouthpiece	*boquilha*	*boo-kee-llea*
pipe	*cachimbo*	*cashinboo*
smoking	*fumar*	*foomar*
tobacco	*tabaco*	*tabacoo*

3.4.3. Big stores

Where is the ladies' department, juniors', children's, men's?	*Onde fica a secção de senhora, jovem, infantil, de homem?*	*Ond feeca a seksowng the senhyora, jovain, infanteel, the homain.?*
In what floor is the gift department?	*Em que piso fica a secção de artigos para oferta?*	*Ayng ker peezoo feeca a seksowng the arteegoosh para ofairta?*
Where is the ladder, the lift (elevator)?	*Onde é a escada rolante, o elevador?*	*Ond air a eshcada roolante, oo eelevador?*
I would like this gift wrapped, please take the pricetag off.	*Gostaria que embrulhasse para oferecer, retire o preço.*	*Goshtaria ker embroo-lleasse para oferessere, reteere oo priessoo.*
Where is the register, check-off?	*Onde é a caixa?*	*Ond air a Kyeesha?*

Vocabulary

counter	*balcão*	*balcaowng*
fitting room	*cabina de provas*	*cabeena the provash*
floor	*piso*	*peezoo*

ground floor	rés-do-chão	raish doo shaowng
lift, elevator	elevador	eelevador
moving staircase	escada rolante	eshcada roolante
package	embrulho	embroolhoo
register	caixa	kyeesha
section	secção	seksowng
shelves	estante	eshtante
window	montra	montra

3.4.3.1. Clothes

I would like to try on this suit, these pants, this skirt...	Queria experimentar este fato, estas calças, esta saia...	Kria eshpereementar eshte fatoo, estash calssash, eshta syea...
My size is...	A minha medida é...	A mee-gna medeeda air...
Could I try it on?	Posso experimentar?	Possoo eshpereementar?
Do you have this skirt in a lighter, darker, colour?	Tem esta saia num tom mais claro, escuro?	Tayng eshta syea noom tom mysh claroo, eshcooroo?
I like this one, although it's narrow, wide, big, tight.	Gosto deste, mas fica-me apertado, largo, grande, justo.	Goshtoo deshte, mash feeca-mer apertadoo, largo, grande, jooshtoo.
Do you have a bigger, smaller, size?	Tem um tamanho maior, menor?	Tayng oom ta-ma-gnoo mayor, menor?

Could you take my measurements?	Poderia ver quais são as minhas medidas?	Pooderia ver kuaysh saowng ash meegnash medeedash?
Could you do some alterations?	Fazem arranjos?	Fazain arranjoosh?
How many days will it take?	Quantos dias demora?	Kwantoosh deeash demora?
I need it by...	Vou precisar da roupa para...	Vou preseezar da roupa para...
Could you show me that print fabric?	Pode mostrar-me aquele tecido estampado?	Pod mooshtrar-mer akierle teseedoo eshtampadoo?
Is it cotton, wool...?	É de algodão, lã...?	Air the algoodowng, lan...?
Where are the fitting rooms?	Onde fica a cabina de provas?	Ond feeca a cabeena the provash?

Vocabulary

Garments	Vestuário	Vesh-too-aryoo
belt	cinto	sentoo
blouse	blusa	blooza
bra	soutien	sootiene
buckle	fivela	feevela
button	botão	botaowng
coat	casaco	cazacoo

dress	*vestido*	*veshteedoo*
gabardine	*gabardina*	*gabardeena*
girdle	*cinta*	*seenta*
gloves	*luvas*	*loovash*
handkerchief	*lenço*	*lenssoo*
hat	*chapéu*	*shapeoo*
hunting shirt	*camuflado*	*camoofladoo*
jacket	*jaqueta*	*jackearta*
jeans	*calças de ganga*	*calsash the ganga*
overcoat	*sobretudo*	*sobretoodoo*
panties	*calções*	*calsoynsh*
pants	*calças*	*calsash*
raincoat	*impermeável*	*impermeeavel*
robe	*roupão*	*ropaowng*
scarf	*cachecol*	*cashecol*
shirt	*camisa*	*cameeza*
shoes	*sapatos*	*sapatoosh*
skirt	*saia*	*syea*
slip	*combinação*	*combeenasowng*
slip	*saiote*	*syeote*
socks	*peúgas*	*peoogash*
stockings	*meias*	*mayash*
sweater	*pulôver*	*pullover*
swimsuit	*fato de banho*	*fatoo the baygnoo*

t-shirt	*camisola*	*cameezola*
tie	*gravata*	*gravata*
underpants	*cuecas*	*cooecash*
underwear	*roupa interior*	*roupa intereeor*
vest	*colete*	*coolete*
zipper	*fecho*	*fayshoo*

Fabrics	*Tecidos*	*Teceedoosh*
acrylic	*acrílico*	*akreeleecoo*
corduroy	*bombazina*	*bombazeena*
cotton	*algodão*	*algoodowng*
felt	*feltro*	*feltroo*
flannel	*flanela*	*flanela*
knitted	*malha*	*mylha*
lace	*renda*	*renda*
leather	*cabedal*	*kabedal*
leather	*couro*	*couroo*
nylon	*nylon*	*nylon*
satin	*cetim*	*seteen*
silk	*seda*	*seda*
thread	*fio*	*feeoo*
velvet	*veludo*	*veloodoo*
wool	*lã*	*lan*

3.4.3.2. Shoes

I would like a pair of... shoes, made of leather, with a leather sole, rubber.	*Quero um par de sapatos, de cor..., de pele, com sola de couro, de borracha.*	*Keroo oom par the sapatoosh, the core..., the pell, con sola the couro,the boorrasha.*
What size do you wear?	*Que número calça?*	*Ker noomeroo calssa?*
My size is forty one.	*O meu número é o 41.*	*Oo meoo noomeroo air kwuarenta ee oom.*
When can I pick them up?	*Quando posso vir buscá-los?*	*Kwandoo possoo veer booshcaloosh?*
Could you give me half-soles?	*Pode colocar-lhes meias-solas?*	*Pod cooloocarllesh mayash solash?*
They are a little small, narrow, wide, somewhat big.	*Ficam-me um pouco pequenos, apertados, largos, um pouco grandes.*	*Ficowng-mer oom poucoo pekiernoosh, apertadoosh, largoosh, oom poucoo grandesh.*
Would you have this same shoe in another color?	*Tem este modelo noutra cor?*	*Tayng eshte moodeloo noutra core?*
Do you have a larger, smaller, size of this same shoe?	*Tem um número maior, mais pequeno, com o mesmo modelo?*	*Tayng oom noomeroo mayeor, mysh pekiernoo, con oo meshmoo modeloo?*
Could you show me those boots, the ones on the window?	*Pode mostrar-me aquelas botas que estão expostas na montra?*	*pod mooshtrar-mer akairlash botash ker eshtowng eshposhtash na montra?*

| Could you fix the heel of this shoe? | *Pode arranjar-me o salto do sapato?* | *Pod arranjar-mer oo saltoo doo sapatoo?* |
| I need a little polish, brown, black, shoestrings. | *Queria um pouco de graxa, uns atacadores castanhos, pretos.* | *Kria oom poucoo the grasha, oonsh atacadoresh cash-ta-gnoosh, priertoosh.* |

Vocabulary

boots	*botas*	*botash*
buckle	*fivela*	*feevela*
cords	*atacadores*	*atacadoresh*
foot	*pé*	*pair*
heel	*salto*	*saltoo*
insole	*palmilha*	*palmeella*
leather	*couro*	*couro*
polish	*graxa*	*grasha*
rubber	*borracha*	*boorrasha*
sandal	*sandália*	*sandaleea*
shoe	*sapato*	*sapatoo*
shoehorn	*calçadeira*	*calssadayra*
size	*medida*	*medeeda*
slippers	*chinelas*	*sheenelash*
sole	*sola*	*sola*

City

3.5. Leisure, tourism and sports

3.5.1. Tourism

Where is the tourist office?	*Onde fica o posto de turismo?*	*Ond feeca oo poshtoo the tooreeshmoo?*
What are the most important artistic monuments of this city?	*Quais são os monumentos artísticos mais importantes da cidade?*	*Kwysh sowng oosh monoomentoosh arteeshteecoosh mysh impoortantesh da seedad?*
How much is the excursion?	*Qual é o preço da excursão?*	*Kwal air oo prierssoo da eshcoorsowng?*
Do you have a city map, a map of the surrounding areas?	*Tem um mapa da cidade, dos arredores?*	*Tayng oom mapa da seedad, doosh arredoresh?*
Is there an organized tour to visit the old city?	*Existe algum percurso turístico organizado para visitar a cidade antiga?*	*Ezeeshte algoom percoorssoo tooreeshteecoo organeezado para veezeetar a seedad anteega?*
When does it start and when does it finish?	*A que horas começa e a que horas acaba?*	*Er ker orash coomairssa ee a ker orash acaba?*
Where is the Parliament, the cathedral, the church of...?	*Onde fica o parlamento, a catedral, a igreja de...?*	*Ond feeca oo parlamentoo, a katedral, a eegrayja the...?*
What church is this?	*Como se chama esta igreja?*	*Komoo ser shama eshta eegrayja?*

City

I would like to visit... How much time does it take to walk there?	*Desejava visitar... A pé, quanto tempo se demora?*	*Dezejava veezeetar... a pair, kwantoo tempoo ser demora?*
What period and style does it belong to?	*De que época é e de que estilo?*	*The ker epooca air ee the ker esteeloo?*
What artistic movement is it?	*A que estilo artístico pertence?*	*Er ker eshteeloo arteeshteecoo pertensse?*
Can one climb the tower?	*É possível subir à torre?*	*Air posseevel soobeer a torre?*

Vocabulary

abbey	*abadia*	*abadeea*
agency	*agência*	*ajencia*
apse	*abside*	*abseede*
aquarium	*aquário*	*ackwareeo*
arcades	*arcadas*	*arcadash*
architecture	*arquitectura*	*arkeytairtoora*
art	*arte*	*arte*
art gallery	*galeria de arte*	*galeria the arte*
avenue	*avenida*	*aveneeda*
bag	*mala, bolsa*	*mala, bolssa*
bank	*banco*	*bancoo*
barracks	*quartel*	*kwartel*
basilica	*basílica*	*bazzeeleeca*

bath	*balneário*	*balne-are-reeo*
bridge	*ponte*	*pont*
building	*edifício*	*edeefeeceeoo*
capital	*capital*	*capeetal*
capital	*capitel*	*capeetell*
castle	*castelo*	*cashtairloo*
cathedral	*catedral*	*catedral*
cemetery	*cemitério*	*cemeetairioo*
center	*centro*	*centro*
chapel	*capela*	*capairla*
church	*igreja*	*eegrayja*
cinema	*cinema*	*seenema*
city	*cidade*	*seedad*
city council	*câmara municipal*	*camara mooneeseepal*
city map	*mapa da cidade*	*mapa da seedad*
civilization	*civilização*	*see-vee-lee-za-sowng*
cloister	*claustro*	*cloushtroo*
column	*coluna*	*cooloona*
construction	*construção*	*conshtroosowng*
contamination	*poluição*	*polooeesowng*
convent	*convento*	*conventoo*
corner	*esquina*	*eskeena*
craft	*artesanato*	*artezanatoo*

decoration	*decoração*	*decoorasowng*
district	*bairro*	*byrroo*
dome	*cúpula*	*coopoola*
era	*época*	*airpooca*
establishment	*estabelecimento*	*eshtabeleseementoo*
exhibition	*exposição*	*eshpoozeesowng*
façade	*fachada*	*far-shah-dar*
factory	*fábrica*	*fabreeca*
fair	*feira*	*fayra*
file	*arquivo*	*arkeyvoo*
fortress	*fortaleza*	*foortalearza*
fountain	*fonte*	*font*
garbage	*lixo*	*leeshoo*
garden	*jardim*	*jardin*
hospital	*hospital*	*oshpeetal*
lake	*lago*	*lagoo*
landscape	*paisagem*	*payssarjane*
market	*mercado*	*mercadoo*
monastery	*mosteiro*	*mooshtayroo*
monument	*monumento*	*monoomentoo*
mosaic	*mosaico*	*moozycoo*
mural	*fresco*	*freshcoo*
museum	*museu*	*moozeu*
nave	*nave*	*narve*
old	*antigo*	*anteegoo*

palace	*palácio*	*palarseeoo*
panoramic view	*vista panorâmica*	*veeshta panorameeca*
park	*parque*	*park*
patio	*pátio*	*pateoo*
pavilion	*pavilhão*	*paveelaowng*
pool	*piscina*	*peeshseena*
portico	*pórtico*	*porteecoo*
residence	*residência*	*rezeedenceea*
river	*rio*	*reeoo*
rose window	*rosácea*	*roozarseea*
ruins	*ruínas*	*rueenash*
school	*escola*	*eshcola*
sculpture	*escultura*	*eshcooltoora*
sidewalk	*passeio*	*passayoo*
square	*praça*	*prarssa*
stadium	*estádio*	*eshtadeeo*
stain glass window	*vitral*	*veetral*
statue	*estátua*	*eshtatooa*
steeple	*campanário*	*campanareeo*
style	*estilo*	*eshteeloo*
surroundings	*arredores*	*arredoresh*
street	*rua*	*rua*
tablet	*lápide*	*lapeede*
terrace	*terraço*	*terrassoo*

theater	*teatro*	*teatroo*
vault	*abóboda*	*abobada*
wall	*parede*	*parede*
walls	*muralhas*	*mooralhash*
wastepaper basket	*cesto de papéis*	*seshtoo the papaysh*
window	*montra*	*montra*
zoo	*jardim zoológico*	*jardin zoologicoo*

3.5.1.1. Museums

Where is the... museum?	*Onde fica o museu de...?*	*Ond feeca oo moozeu the...?*
How much are the tickets to this museum, exhibition...?	*Quanto custa a entrada neste museu, exposição?*	*Kwantoo cooshta a entrada nesht moozeu, eshpoozeesowng?*
When does it close?	*A que horas encerra?*	*Er Ker orash encerra?*
Can we take pictures?	*Podem tirar-se fotografias?*	*Podain teerar-ser footoografeeash?*
Are there guided visits?	*Há visitas guiadas?*	*Are veeseetash geeadash?*
I would like to buy a catalogue.	*Queria comprar o catálogo.*	*Kria comprar oo catalogoo.*
How long will this exhibition be here?	*Até quando estará patente a exposição?*	*Atair kwandoo eshtarar patente a eshpoozeesowng?*

altarpiece	*retábulo*	*retarbooloo*
armour	*armadura*	*armadoora*
art gallery	*galeria de quadros*	*galeria the kwardroosh*
artist	*artista*	*arteeshta*
bust	*busto*	*booshtoo*
canvas	*tela*	*teller*
catalogue	*catálogo*	*catalogoo*
century	*século*	*saircooloo*
ceramic	*cerâmica*	*cerameeca*
coin	*moeda*	*mooeda*
collection	*colecção*	*colearsowng*
colour	*cor*	*core*
drawing	*desenho*	*dezengno*
entrance	*entrada*	*entrada*
excavations	*escavações*	*eshcavasoynsh*
exhibition	*exposição*	*eshpoozeesowng*
foundation	*fundação*	*fundasowng*
image	*imagem*	*imarjane*
landscape	*paisagem*	*pyszarjane*
lithograph	*litografia*	*letoografeea*
low relief	*baixo-relevo*	*bysho relearvo*
manuscript	*manuscrito*	*manooshcreetoo*
miniature	*miniatura*	*meeneeatoora*

mosaic	*mosaico*	*mosycoo*
mummy	*múmia*	*moomeea*
museum	*museu*	*moozeu*
old	*antigo*	*anteegoo*
painting	*quadro*	*kwardroo*
portrait	*retrato*	*retrartoo*
print	*gravura*	*gravoora*
project	*projecto*	*projetoo*
realism	*realismo*	*reealeeshmoo*
reconstruction	*reconstrução*	*reconshtroosowng*
relief	*relevo*	*relevoo*
reproduction	*reprodução*	*reprodoosowng*
restoration	*restauro*	*reshtauroo*
room	*sala*	*sala*
ruins	*ruínas*	*rooeenash*
sculptor	*escultor*	*eshcooltor*
sculpture	*escultura*	*eshtartooa*
statue	*estátua*	*eshcooltoora*
still life	*natureza-morta*	*natooreza morta*
style	*estilo*	*eshteeloo*
tapestry	*tapete*	*tapearte*
time	*época*	*airpooca*
visit	*vista*	*veezeeta*
visitors	*visitantes*	*veezeetantesh*

Art	Arte	Arte
abstract	*abstracta*	*abshtrata*
arabic	*árabe*	*arabe*
baroque	*barroca*	*barrohca*
contemporary	*contemporânea*	*contemporaneea*
cubist	*cubista*	*coobeeshta*
expressionist	*expressionista*	*eshpre-seeyou-neeshta*
gothic	*gótica*	*goteeca*
greek	*grega*	*grega*
impressionist	*impressionista*	*impre-seeyou-neeshta*
modern	*moderna*	*mooderna*
neoclassicist	*neoclássica*	*neoclaseeca*
realist	*realista*	*realeeshta*
renaissance	*renascentista*	*renascenteeshta*
roman	*romana*	*romana*
romanic	*românica*	*romaneeca*
romantic	*romântica*	*romanteeca*

3.5.1.2. Theater and cinema

What is playing at the cinema, showing at the theatre, this afternoon, tonight?	*O que está em exibição no cinema, teatro, esta tarde, noite?*	*Oo ker eshtar ayng eshpoozeesowng noo seenema, teatroo, eshta tard, noyt?*

Are there any tickets available for tonight's show?	*Ainda há bilhetes para o espectáculo desta noite?*	*Ainda are beelletesh para oo eshpair-tacooloo deshta noyt?*
Is the film dubbed?	*O filme é dobrado?*	*Oo feelm air doobradoo?*
When does the play start?	*A que horas começa a peça?*	*Er ker orash coomairssa a pairssa?*
Where can you get tickets?	*Onde se pode adquirir os bilhetes?*	*Ond ser pod adkeyrir osh beelletesh?*
I would like to reserve some tickets for...	*Desejava reservar bilhetes para...*	*Dezejava rezervar beelletesh para...*
Could I have a program, please?	*Pode dar-me um programa, por favor?*	*Pod dar-mer oom prooograma, poor favor?*
What is the program for tonight's concert?	*Qual é o programa para o concerto desta tarde?*	*Kwal air o programa para oo concertoo deshta tard?*
I would like to reserve two seats in the balcony.	*Queria reservar dois lugares para o balcão.*	*Kria rezervar doysh loogaresh para oo balcaowng.*
I'm sorry, it's sold out.	*Lamento, os bilhetes estão esgotados.*	*Lamentoo, oosh beelhetesh eshtaowng eshgootardoosh.*

Theater, cinema	*Teatro, cinema*	*Teeatroo, cinema*
acoustics	*acústica*	*acooshteeca*
act	*acto*	*atoo*
actor	*actor*	*ator*
actress	*actriz*	*atreesh*
animated cartoons	*desenhos animados*	*dezegnhoosh aneemadoosh*
applause	*aplausos*	*aplauzoosh*
ballet	*bailado*	*bylardoo*
box office	*bilheteira*	*belletayra*
character	*personagem*	*perssonarjane*
cinema	*cinema*	*seenema*
circus	*circo*	*circoo*
comedy	*comédia*	*coomairdeea*
curtain	*pano de cena*	*panoo the sena*
direction	*realização*	*realeezasoung*
documentary	*documentário*	*do-coomenta-ree-oo*
director	*encenador*	*encenador*
drama	*drama*	*drama*
dressing room	*camarim*	*camarin*
dubbing	*dobragem*	*doobrarjane*
editing	*montagem*	*montarjane*
end	*fim*	*feen*

entrance	*entrada*	*entrada*
exit	*saída*	*saeeda*
festival	*festival*	*feshteeval*
figuration	*figuração*	*feegoorasowng*
film	*longa-metragem*	*longa metrarjane*
gallery	*galeria*	*galeria*
hooters	*assobios*	*assobeeoosh*
interpretation	*interpretação*	*inter-pre-ta-saowng*
interval	*intervalo*	*intervarloo*
lobby	*vestíbulo*	*veshteebooloo*
marionettes	*marionetas*	*mareeonairtash*
movie	*filme*	*feelm*
opera	*ópera*	*opera*
operetta	*zarzuela*	*zarzooairla*
play	*peça*	*pairssa*
plot	*trama*	*trama*
poster	*cartaz*	*cartash*
premiere	*estreia*	*eshtraya*
program	*programa*	*proograma*
projection	*projecção*	*proojairsowng*
projector	*projector*	*proojairtor*
protagonist	*protagonista*	*prootagooneeshta*
public	*público*	*poobleecoo*
puppets	*fantoches*	*fantoshesh*
queue	*fila de espera*	*feela the eshpaira*

representation	representação	reprezentasowng
reservation	reserva	rezairva
scene	cena	sena
scenery	cenário	senarrio
screen	ecrã	ekcran
script	guião	gueeowng
season	temporada	tempoorada
seat	assento	acentoo
set	cenografia	senoografeea
setting	lugar	loogar
short film	curta-metragem	coorta metrarjane
show	espectáculo	eshpairtarcooloo
soundtrack	banda sonora	banda soonora
spectator	espectador	eshpairtador
stage	palco	palcoo
text	texto	teshtoo
theater	teatro	teatroo
ticket	bilhete	beellet
time	tempo	tempoo
title	título	teetooloo
tragedy	tragédia	trajairdeea
twins	binóculos	beenocooloosh
usher	arrumador	arroomador
voice	voz	vosh
wardrobe	vestuário	veshtooarrio

wardrobes	*guarda-roupa*	*guarda-roupa*
wings	*bastidores*	*bashteeduresh*
work	*obra*	*obra*

Opera, concerts, ballet	*Ópera, concertos, bailado*	*Opra, consertoosh, bylardoo*
aria	*aria*	*areea*
ballerina	*bailarina*	*bylareena*
ballet	*bailado*	*bylardoo*
band	*banda*	*banda*
baton	*batuta*	*batoota*
bolero	*bolero*	*boolairoo*
choreography	*coreografia*	*cooreeografeea*
choir	*coro*	*coro*
composer	*compositor*	*compoozeetour*
composition	*composição*	*compoozeesowng*
concert	*concerto*	*concerto*
concert hall	*sala de concertos*	*sala the concertoosh*
dance	*dança*	*danssa*
dancer	*bailarino*	*bylareenoo*
duet	*duo*	*doo*
group	*grupo*	*groopoo*
interpreter	*intérprete*	*intairprete*

orchestra	*orquestra*	*orkairshtra*
overture	*abertura*	*abertoora*
phillarmonic	*filarmónica*	*feelarmoneeca*
quartet	*quarteto*	*kwartertoo*
quintet	*quinteto*	*kintertoo*
recital	*recital*	*reseetal*
score	*partitura*	*parteetoora*
show	*espectáculo*	*eshpetarcooloo*
soloist	*solista*	*sooleeshta*
sonata	*sonata*	*sonata*
song	*canto*	*cantoo*
sound	*som*	*son*
study	*estúdio*	*eshtoodeeoo*
symphony	*sinfonia*	*sinfooneea*
trio	*trio*	*treeoo*
waltz	*valsa*	*valssa*

Singers	Cantores	Can-toh-resh
baritone	*barítono*	*bareetoonoo*
bass	*baixo*	*byshoo*
contralto	*contralto*	*contraaltoo*
mezzo soprano	*meio-soprano*	*mayoo-soopranoo*
soprano	*soprano*	*soopranoo*
tenor	*tenor*	*tenor*

Music	Música	Moo-see-ka
chamber	de câmara	the camara
classical	clássica	clarseeca
contemporary	contemporânea	contemporaneea
jazz	jazz	jazz
modern	moderna	moodairna
old	antiga	anteega
pop	pop	pop
rock	rock	rock
sacred	sacra	sacra
symphonic	sinfónica	sinforneeca

Instruments	Instrumentos	Inshtroo-mentosh
accordion	acordeão	acordeeowng
bassoon	fagote	fagorte
battery, drums	bateria	batereea
cello	violoncelo	veeoolonsairloo
clarinet	clarinete	clareenete
contrabass	contrabaixo	contrabyshoo
cymbals	pratos	pratoosh
drum	tambor	tambor
flute	flauta	flaoota
guitar	guitarra	guitarrra
harp	harpa	aarpa

mandolin	*bandolim*	*bandoolin*
oboe	*oboé*	*obooair*
piano	*piano*	*peeanoo*
saxophone	*saxofone*	*saxofon*
trombone	*trombone*	*trombon*
trumpet	*trompete*	*trompairte*
viola	*viola*	*veeorla*
violin	*violino*	*veeooleenoo*

Club	*Discoteca*	*Dees-koo-te-ka*
bar	*bar*	*bar*
consumption	*consumo*	*consoomoo*
counter	*balcão*	*balcowng*
dancing	*dançar*	*danssar*
danse	*dança*	*danssa*
drink	*bebida*	*bebeeda*
entrance	*entrada*	*entrarda*
musical group	*grupo musical*	*groopoo moozeecal*
partner	*acompanhante*	*acom-pa-gnant*
party hall	*salão de festas*	*salaowng the feshtash*
reservation	*reserva*	*rezairva*
show	*espectáculo*	*eshpairtacooloo*
singer	*cantor*	*cantor*
table	*mesa*	*mairza*
toast	*brinde*	*breend*
waiter	*empregado*	*empregardoo*

3.5.1.3. Sports

Could you tell me if there is a football, basketball, tennis match on today?	*Poderia dizer-me se hoje há jogo de futebol, de basquetebol, ténis?*	*Pooderia deezair-mer ser oje are jogoo the footeboll, the bashketboll, tairneesh?*
What teams are playing?	*Que equipas jogam?*	*Ker ekeypash jogowng?*
Where is the football field?	*Onde fica o campo de futebol?*	*Ond feeca oo campo the footeboll?*
When does the game start?	*A que horas começa o encontro?*	*Er ker orash coomairssa oo encontroo?*
How much is the ticket for the event, the race, the game?	*Quanto custa a entrada para o evento, a corrida, o encontro?*	*Kwantoo cooshta a entrarda para oo eeventoo, a coorreeda, oo encontroo?*
Is there a pool or a club around here?	*Há alguma piscina ou clube nesta zona?*	*Are algooma peeshseena or cloobe neshta zonah?*
Can you swim in this river, lake?	*Pode tomar-se banho neste rio, lago?*	*Pod toomar-ser baygnoo neshte reeo, largoo?*
Could you tell me where the car races, motorcycle, bycicle, are held?	*Poderia dizer-me onde se fazem as corridas de carros, de motos, de bicicleta?*	*Poodeia deezair-mer ond ser farzain ash coorreedash the carroosh, the mortoosh, the beeseeclairta?*
Where is the horse track?	*Onde fica o hipódromo?*	*Ond feeca oo eepordroomoo?*

| Where can you place bets, in the horse track? | *A que zona do hipódromo me devo dirigir para fazer apostas?* | *Er ker zonah doo eepor-droomoo mer dearvoo dee-ree-geer para fazair aporshtash?* |
| I would like to ride a bycicle. | *Queria passear de bicicleta.* | *Kria passeear the beeseeclairta.* |

Vocabulary

athlete	*atleta*	*atlairta*
ball	*bola*	*borla*
basket	*cesto*	*sesh-too*
bicycle	*bicicleta*	*beeseeclairta*
boat	*barco*	*barcoo*
champion	*campeão*	*campeeaowng*
classification	*classificação*	*kla-sse-fee-ka-sowng*
competition	*competição*	*competeesowng*
craft	*embarcação*	*embarcasowng*
disqualifying	*desqualificar*	*desh-kwa-lee-feecar*
escalade	*escalada*	*eshcalarda*
fan	*aficionado*	*afeeseeonardoo*
finalist	*finalista*	*feenaleeshta*
fishing	*pesca*	*pairshca*
fishing license	*licença de pesca*	*leesenssa the pairshca*
fishing rod	*cana de pesca*	*cana the pairshca*
football field	*campo de futebol*	*campoo the footeboll*
footballer	*futebolista*	*foote-boo-leeshta*
game	*partida*	*parteeda*

goal	*baliza*	*baleeza*
goal	*meta*	*mairta*
goal keeper	*guarda-redes*	*guarda rairdesh*
gym	*ginásio*	*geenarzeeoo*
helm	*timão, leme*	*teemaowng, lairmer*
hunt	*caçar*	*cahssar*
hunter	*caçador*	*cassador*
jump	*salto*	*saltoo*
marathon	*maratona*	*maratona*
medal	*medalha*	*medarllea*
net	*rede*	*rearde*
oar	*remo*	*rearmoo*
olympics	*olimpíada*	*oleenpeeada*
player	*jogador*	*joogador*
pool	*piscina*	*peeshseena*
race	*corrida*	*coorreeda*
race track	*hipódromo*	*eepordroomoo*
racket	*raquete*	*rakairter*
record	*record*	*raircord*
referee	*árbitro*	*arbeetroo*
rowing	*remar*	*remahre*
runner	*corredor*	*corredor*
shotgun	*espingarda*	*eshpingarda*
skates	*patins*	*pateensh*
ski	*esqui*	*eshkey*
sport	*desporto*	*deshportoo*
sport discipline	*disciplina*	*deesh-see-pleena*
	desportiva	*desh-poor-teeva*

stables	*cavalariças*	*cavalareessash*
stadium	*estádio*	*eshtardeeo*
summit	*cume*	*coome*
team	*equipa*	*eekeypa*
tennis court	*campo de ténis*	*campoo the tairneesh*
test	*prova*	*prorva*
tie, draw	*empate*	*emparte*
tiing	*empatar*	*empatar*
time	*tempo*	*tempoo*
to lose	*perder*	*perder*
to ride	*montar*	*montar*
track	*pista*	*peeshta*
trainer	*treinador*	*traynador*
training	*treino*	*traynoo*
track field	*velódremo*	*velordroomoo*
trip	*excursão*	*escoorsowng*
untie	*desempate*	*dezenparte*
wardrobe	*vestiário*	*vestuareeoo*

Sports	***Desportos***	*Desh-por-toosh*
athletics	*atletismo*	*atlairteeshmoo*
baseball	*basebol*	*bayzeboll*
basketball	*basquetebol*	*bashketboll*
boxing	*boxe*	*box*
cycling	*ciclismo*	*seecleeshmoo*
discus throwing	*lançamento do disco*	*lanssamentoo do deeshcoo*

fencing	*esgrima*	eshgreema
fishing	*pesca*	pairshca
football	*futebol*	footeboll
free fight	*luta livre*	loota leevree
golf	*golfe*	golfe
gymnastics	*ginástica*	geenarshteeca
handball	*andebol*	andeboll
hockey	*hóquei*	ohkey
horsemanship	*equitação*	ekeytasowng
hunting	*caça*	carssa
javelin	*dardo*	dardoo
judo	*judo*	joodoo
karate	*karaté*	carartair
motorcycling	*motociclismo*	motoseecleeshmoo
mountaineering	*alpinismo*	alpeeneeshmoo
ping-pong	*pingue-pongue*	ping pong
polo	*pólo*	porloo
races	*corrida de cavalos*	correeda the cavarloosh
rowing	*remo*	rearmoo
rugby	*râguebi*	rayguerbee
skating	*patinagem*	pateenarjane
ski	*esqui*	eshkey
swimming	*natação*	natasowng
target pratice	*tiro*	teeroo
tennis	*ténis*	tairneesh
volleyball	*voleibol*	vorleyboll
weight lifting	*halterofilia*	altair-ror-fee-leea

3.5.1.4. Beach, mountains and countryside

Could you tell me where can I find a quiet beach?	*Poderia indicar-me uma praia tranquila?*	*Podereea indeecar-mer ooma pryeea trankweela?*
Where can I rent a beach umbrella and a lawn chair, please?	*Onde poderei alugar um guarda-sol e cadeiras de praia, por favor?*	*Ond pooderay aloogar oom guarda sol ee cadayrash the pryeea, poor favor?*
Is it safe to swim on this beach?	*Pode-se nadar sem perigo nesta praia?*	*Porde ser nadar sain pereegoo neshta pryeea?*
Where can I rent a boat?	*Onde posso alugar um barco?*	*Ond possoo aloogar oom barcoo?*
Are there any dangerous currents?	*Há alguma corrente perigosa?*	*Are algooma coorrente pereegorza?*
The water is cold, hot, clean, dirty, muddy.	*A água está fria, quente, limpa, suja, turva.*	*A argua eshtar freea, Kiernt, leempa, sooja toorva.*
Is the nearest town very far?	*A localidade mais próxima é muito longe daqui?*	*A loocaleedad mysh prorseema air moitoo longe dakey?*
We would like to take an excursion around the mountains. Do you have a map of the roads, inns, trails?	*Queríamos fazer uma excursão pela montanha. Tem algum mapa de caminhos, albergues, carreiros?*	*Kerermoosh fazear ooma eshcoorsowng pela mon-ta-gna. Tayng algoom mapa the ca-mee-gnoosh, albairguesh, car-ray-roosh?*

Do these mountains have refuges where one can spend the night?	*Estas montanhas têm refúgio onde se possa passar a noite?*	*Eshtash montangnash taynghem refoogeeooosh ond ser porssa passar a noyt?*
I would like to rent mountaineering equipment, ski equipment.	*Gostaria de alugar equipamento de montanha, de esqui.*	*Gooshtaria the aloogar ekeypamentoo the mon-ta-gna, the eshkey.*
Is there any typical celebration in the towns of this area?	*Há alguma festa típica nesta região?*	*Are algooma fairshta neshta regeeaowng?*

Vocabulary

air	*ar*	*ahr*
algae	*algas*	*algash*
animal	*animal*	*aneemal*
backpack	*mochila*	*moosheela*
balneary	*balneário*	*balneareeo*
barrier	*cerca*	*serca*
basin	*tanque*	*tank*
bath	*banho*	*bay-gnoo*
bay	*enseada*	*enseearda*
bay	*baía*	*baeea*
beach	*praia*	*pryeea*
bird	*pássaro*	*parssaroo*
boat	*barco*	*bahrcoo*
boots	*botas*	*bortash*

bridge	*ponte*	*pont*
camping	*acampar*	*acampar*
cane	*bastão*	*bashtaowng*
canteen	*cantil*	*canteel*
cave	*gruta*	*groota*
channel	*canal*	*canal*
cottage	*casa de campo*	*carza the campo*
current	*corrente*	*corrente*
drinkable water	*água potável*	*argua pootarvel*
farm	*quinta*	*keenta*
field	*campo*	*campoo*
fire	*fogo*	*fogoo*
fish	*peixe*	*payshe*
fisherman	*pescador*	*peshcador*
float	*flutuador*	*flootooador*
flock	*rebanho*	*rerbaygno*
forest	*bosque*	*boshker*
forest	*floresta*	*floorearshta*
fountain	*fonte*	*font*
glacier	*glaciar*	*glaseear*
glasses	*óculos*	*ohcooloosh*
grass	*pastagem*	*pashtarjane*
grassland	*prado*	*prardoo*
gulf	*golfo*	*golfoo*
highway	*auto-estrada*	*auto eshtrarda*
hill	*colina*	*cooleena*
house	*casa*	*carza*
hut	*cabana*	*cabana*
ice	*gelo*	*jerloo*

immersion	*imersão*	*eemersowng*
insect	*insecto*	*insairtoo*
island	*ilha*	*ellea*
lake	*lago*	*largo*
landscape	*paisagem*	*paeezarjane*
lantern	*lanterna*	*lantearna*
lawn chair	*trenó*	*trenor*
lifeboat	*salva-vidas*	*salva veedash*
lighthouse	*farol*	*farol*
mountain	*montanha*	*montagna*
nail	*prego*	*prairgoo*
path	*vereda*	*verearda*
pine forest	*pinhal*	*peergnal*
plain	*planície*	*pler-nee-see*
plant	*planta*	*planta*
port-harbour	*porto*	*portoo*
racket	*raqueta*	*rakearta*
reef	*rochedo*	*roosheardoo*
refuge	*refúgio*	*refoogeeoo*
rest	*repouso*	*repouzoo*
rifle	*espingarda*	*eshpeengarda*
river	*rio*	*rio/reeoo*
road	*caminho*	*cameenhoo*
road	*estrada*	*eshtrarda*
rock	*rocha*	*rorsha*
rope	*corda*	*corda*
sand	*areia*	*araya*
sea	*mar*	*mahr*
seat	*cadeira*	*cadayra*

sled	*cadeira de repouso*	cadayra the repouzoo
shell	*concha*	consha
shower	*duche*	dooshe
skate	*patins*	patinsh
sky	*céu*	saioo
snow	*neve*	nairve
spring	*nascente*	nashente
stable	*estábulo*	eshtarbooloo
star	*estrela*	eshtrerla
stream	*regato*	regartoo
stone	*pedra*	pairdra
summit	*cume*	coome
sun	*sol*	sol
sunset	*pôr do sol*	por doo sol
suntan	*bronzeado*	bronzeeardoo
swimming	*natação*	natasowng
to dive	*mergulhar*	mergoollear
torrent	*torrente*	toorente
tree	*árvore*	arvoore
trip	*excursão*	eshcoorsowng
vacation, holiday	*férias*	fairreeash
valley	*vale*	varle
view	*panorama*	panorama
village	*aldeia*	aldayeea
vineyard	*vinha*	veegna
walk	*passeio*	pasayeeoo
wave	*onda*	onda
wind	*vento*	ventoo

4. Health

4.1. Medicine

I need to see a doctor.	*Necessito de um médico.*	*Nesserseetoo the oom mairdeecoo*
When does the doctor see patients? It's urgent!	*Qual é o horário das consultas? É urgente!*	*Kwal air oo orar-rio dash consooltash? Air oorgente!*
What symptoms do you have?	*Quais são os seus sintomas?*	*Kwaysh sowng oosh seroosh senthomash?*
I'm not feeling well.	*Não me estou a sentir bem.*	*Nowng mer eshtour a senteer bain?*
I haven't been able to sleep all night.	*Não consegui dormir durante toda a noite.*	*Nowng conserguee doormeer doorante toda a noyt.*
I feel sick, I have a headache, stomach ache, my throat hurts, my ears hurt.	*Tenho vontade de vomitar, dor de cabeça, estômago, garganta, ouvidos.*	*Tay-gnoo vontarde the voomeetar, dor the cabearssa, the eshtomagoo,garganta, ouveedoosh.*
I'm about to give birth.	*Estou a entrar em trabalho de parto.*	*Eshtour a entrahr em traballeo the partoo.*
I think I have a fever, indigestion.	*Creio estar com febre, com uma indigestão.*	*Krayeeoo eshtar con fairbre, con ooma inder-gesh-towng*
Where does it hurt?	*Onde lhe dói?*	*Ond lher doyee?*

It hurts here, I have... symptoms.	*Dói-me aqui, estou com sintomas de...*	*Doyee-mer akey, eshtour con sinthomash the...*
I think I have broken my arm, my ankle.	*Creio que parti um braço, um tornozelo.*	*Krayeeoo ker partee oom brarssoo,oom toornoozearloo*
I feel dizzy.	*Estou com náuseas.*	*Eshtour con nauzeeash.*
I feel a lot of pressure on my chest.	*Sinto uma forte pressão no peito.*	*Sintoo ooma fort pressowng noo paytoo.*
He's fallen and hurt his head.	*Ele caiu e feriu-se na cabeça.*	*Erlle caeeoo ee ferreoo-ser na cabearssa.*
Take your clothes off, raise your sleeve, please.	*Dispa-se, arregace a manga, por favor.*	*Deeshpasser arregarsse a manga, poor favor.*
How often should I take them?	*De quanto em quanto tempo os devo tomar?*	*The kwantoo ayng kwantoo tempoo oosh dearvoo toomar?*
Open your mouth, close your hand, straighten out your body.	*Abra a boca, feche a mão, estique o corpo.*	*Abra a boca, fayshe a mowng, eshteeker oo corpoo.*
Take a deep breath.	*Respire fundo.*	*Reshpeere fuoondoo.*
I'm going to give you an injection.	*Vou dar-lhe uma injecção.*	*Vou dar-ller ooma injairsowng.*
I'm going to take your pressure, temperature.	*Vou medir-lhe a tensão arterial, a temperatura.*	*Vou medeer-ller a tensowng artereeal, a temperatoora.*

Health

It's nothing serious. Rest a few days and take these medicines.	*Não tem nada de grave. Descanse uns dias e tome estes medicamentos.*	Nowng taiyng narda the grarve. deshcanser oonsh deeash ee tormer ershtersh medeecamentoosh.
Before or after meals, on an empty stomach?	*Antes ou depois das refeições, em jejum?*	Antesh or depoysh dash refaysonynsh, ayng jerjoon?
I have had a heart attack, I have been operated in my...	*Tive um enfarte, um ataque de coração, fui operado a...*	Teeve oom enfarte, oom atarker the coorasowng.fooee operardoo er...
I have hypertension, allergies to antibiotics, to penicillin...	*Sou hipertenso, alérgico aos antibióticos, à penicilina...*	Sore eepair-tensoo, alairgeecoo ow-oosh anteebeeorteecoosh,are perneeceeleena...
We have to bandage your cut, your ankle.	*Temos de lhe ligar a ferida, o tornozelo.*	Termoosh the ller leegar a fereeda oo toornoozairloo.
I'm pregnant.	*Estou grávida.*	Eshtour grarveeda.
I need you to check my vision.	*Preciso que me examine a vista.*	Preseezoo ker mer eezameener a veeshta.
How much do I owe you?	*Quanto lhe devo?*	Kwantoo ller dervoo?
You need to check yourself into a hospital, go to the hospital to have some x-rays taken, check up, analysis.	*Você devia ser hospitalizado, ir ao hospital para que lhe façam radiografias, um exame, análises.*	Vorsear deveea ser oshpeetaleezardoo, eer ow oshpeetal para ker ller farsowng radeeografeeash, oom eezame, anarleezeesh.

Could you give me local anesthesia?	*Pode dar-me uma anestesia local?*	*Pod dar-mer ooma aneshterzeea loocal?*
You need to have your appendix operated on.	*Você precisa de ser operado ao apêndice.*	*Vorsear preseeza the ser operardoo ow apendeese.*
My teeth hurt very much. Do you have an analgesic?	*Estou com muitas dores de dentes. Tem um analgésico?*	*Eshtour con mooeetash doresh the dentesh. Tayng algoom analjairzeecoo?*
I have to take out a tooth.	*Tenho de lhe tirar um dente.*	*Taygnhoo the ller teerar oom dente.*

Vocabulary

Medicine	*Medicina*	*Med-cee-nar*
acidity	*acidez*	*aseedesh*
allergy	*alergia*	*alergeea*
anemia	*anemia*	*anemeea*
anesthesia	*anestesia*	*aneshtezeea*
angina	*anginas*	*angeenahs*
appendicittis	*apendicite*	*apendeeseete*
arthritis	*artrite*	*artreete*
asthma	*asma*	*ashma*
attack	*ataque*	*atarker*
bite	*mordedura*	*moordedoora*
blister	*ampola*	*ampola*

Health

boil	*furúnculo*	*foorooncoolo*
bronchitis	*bronquite*	*bronkeyte*
burn	*queimadura*	*kaymadoora*
chills	*arrepios*	*arrepeeoosh*
cancer	*cancro*	*cancroo*
capsule	*cápsula*	*carpsoola*
caries	*cárie*	*carree*
cold	*catarro*	*catarroo*
cold	*constipação*	*conshteepasowng*
colic	*cólica*	*corleeca*
colitis	*colite*	*corleet*
congestion	*congestão*	*congeshtowng*
constipation	*obstipação*	*obshteepasowng*
cough	*tosse*	*torss*
cramp	*cãibra*	*cayenbra*
cut	*corte*	*corte*
denture	*dentadura*	*dentadoora*
diabetes	*diabetes*	*deeabairtesh*
diarrhea	*diarreia*	*deearaya*
dislocation	*luxação*	*looshasowng*
ear infection	*otite*	*oteet*
exhaustion	*esgotamento*	*eshgootamentoo*
extraction	*extracção*	*estrarsowng*
fainting	*desmaio*	*deshmyoo*
fever	*febre*	*fairbrer*
fracture	*fractura*	*farrtoora*

garglings	*gargarejo*	*gargarayjoo*
gastritis	*gastrite*	*gasgtreet*
gum	*gengiva*	*gengeeva*
headache	*enxaqueca*	*enshakairca*
heart attack	*enfarte*	*enfarte*
heatstroke	*insolação*	*insoolasowng*
hematoma	*hematoma*	*emathoma*
hernia	*hérnia*	*airneea*
illness, disease	*doença*	*dooenssa*
indigestion	*indigestão*	*indegeshtowng*
infection	*infecção*	*infairsowng*
inflammation	*inflamação*	*inflamasowng*
insomnia	*insónia*	*insorneea*
intoxication	*intoxicação*	*intorsheecasowng*
lesion	*lesão*	*lezowng*
lumbago	*lumbago*	*loombargoo*
mouth	*boca*	*bohca*
neck cramp	*torcícolo*	*toorseecorloo*
nerve	*nervo*	*nervoo*
nevralgia	*nevralgia*	*nevralgeea*
pain	*dor*	*dore*
paralysis	*paralisia*	*paraleezeea*
peritonitis	*peritonite*	*pereetooneet*
pharingitis	*faringite*	*faringeeter*
poisoning	*envenenamento*	*envenenamentoo*
pneumonia	*pneumonia*	*pneoomooneea*

Health

prothesis	*prótese*	*protz*
puncture	*pontada*	*pontarda*
sciatica	*ciática*	*seearteeca*
scratch	*arranhão*	*arranhowng*
shock	*choque*	*shock*
sickness	*enjoo*	*enjouo*
sinusitis	*sinusite*	*seenoozeet*
sneeze	*espirro*	*eshpeerroo*
sting	*picada*	*peecarda*
stinging	*escoriação*	*eshcooreeasowng*
stress	*stress*	*stess*
sty	*terçol*	*terssol*
symptoms	*sintomas*	*seenthomash*
tension	*tensão*	*tensowng*
tetanus	*tétano*	*tairtanoo*
throbs	*palpitações*	*palpeetasoyns*
thrombosis	*trombose*	*tromborz*
tooth	*dente*	*dente*
trauma	*traumatismo*	*traumateeshmoo*
tumor	*tumor*	*toomor*
twist	*entorse*	*entorsse*
ulcer	*úlcera*	*ulsera*
varicose veins	*varizes*	*vareezesh*
vertigo	*vertigem*	*verteejane*
vomit	*vómito*	*vormeetoo*
wound	*ferida*	*fereeda*

Illnesses, diseases	Doenças	dooensash
aids	sida	seeda
chicken pox	varicela	vareesairla
ferina cough	tosse convulsa	torss convoolssa
flu, influenza	gripe	greep
hepatitis	hepatite	eparteet
leukemia	leucemia	leocermeea
measles	sarampo	saranpoo
meningitis	meningite	meningeet
pock	varíola	vareeola
poliomyelitis	poliomielite	poleeo-meeairleet
syphilis	sífilis	seefeeleesh
tuberculosis	tuberculose	tourbaircooloz
typhus	tifo	teefoo

Hospital	Hospital	hospital
abortion	aborto	abortoo
ambulance	ambulância	amboolancia
anaesthetic	anestesia	aneshtezeea
analysis	análises	anarleezesh
antitetanic	antitetânico	antitetaneecoo
bed	cama	cama
give birth	dar à luz	dar are loosh
cardiologist	cardiologista	cardeeologeeshta
cast	gesso	jairsso
childbirth	parto	partoo

Health

clinic	*clínica*	*cleeneeca*
consultation	*consulta*	*consoolta*
convalescence	*convalescença*	*convaleshsensa*
cure	*cura*	*coora*
dermatologist	*dermatologista*	*dermatooloogeeshta*
disinfection	*desinfecção*	*desinfairsowng*
epidemic	*epidemia*	*erpeedemeea*
gynecologist	*ginecologista*	*geenaircooloogeeshta*
improvement	*melhora*	*melleora*
infection	*contágio*	*contargeeoo*
intervention	*intervenção*	*intervensowng*
massage	*massagem*	*massarjane*
medication	*medicação*	*medeecasowng*
medication	*medicamento*	*medeecamentoo*
medicine	*medicina*	*medeeseena*
midwife	*parteira*	*partayra*
national health clinic	*ambulatório*	*amboolatoreeo*
nurse	*enfermeira*	*enfermayra*
operation	*operação*	*operasowng*
operating room	*sala de operações*	*sala the operasoyns*
ophthalmologist	*oftalmologista*	*oftalmooloogeeshta*
orthopedic	*ortopedista*	*ortorpedeeshta*
patient	*paciente*	*pasee-ente*
pediatrician	*pediatria*	*pedeeartra*
psychiatrist	*psiquiatria*	*pseekeyatreea*
scalpel	*bisturi*	*beeshtoory*
sick person	*doente*	*dooente*

stretcher	*maca*	*marca*
surgeon	*cirugião*	*seeroogeeowng*
suture	*sutura*	*sootoora*
syringe	*seringa*	*seringa*
therapy	*terapia*	*terapeea*
thermometer	*termómetro*	*termormetroo*
transfusion	*transfusão*	*transhfoosowng*
urgency	*urgência*	*oorgencia*
urologist	*urologista*	*oorooloogeeshta*
vaccine	*vacina*	*vaseena*
x-ray	*radiografia*	*radeeooografeea*

4.2. The pharmacy

Where can I find a chemist?	*Onde posso encontrar uma farmácia?*	*Ond possoo encontrar ooma farmarseea?*
I would like some pills for a cough	*Queria pastilhas para a tosse.*	*Kria pashteelhash para a torss.*
Could you give me an injection?	*Poderia dar-me uma injecção?*	*Poodereea dar-mer ooma injairsowng*
We can't give you this drug without a prescription.	*Não lhe podemos vender este medicamento sem receita médica.*	*Nowng ller poodermoosh vender eshte medeecamentoo sayng resayta mairdeeca*
Do I need a prescription for this drug?	*Vou precisar de receita para adquirir este medicamento?*	*Vour preseezar the resayta para adkeyrir eshte merdeecamentoo?*

alcohol	*álcool*	*alcoo-ol*
analgesic	*analgésico*	*analjairzeecoo*
anti-acid	*antiácido*	*antee-arseedoo*
antibiotic	*antibiótico*	*antee-beeorteecoo*
antidote	*antídoto*	*antee-dootoo*
aspirin	*aspirina*	*ashpeereena*
band-aid	*adesivo*	*adzeevoo*
bandage	*ligadura*	*leegadoora*
bicarbonate	*bicabornato*	*beecarboonartoo*
capsule	*cápsula*	*carpsoola*
chemist	*farmacêutico*	*farma-sseuteecoo*
chemist's shop	*farmácia*	*farmarseea*
compresses	*compressas*	*comprairssash*
contraceptive	*contraceptivo*	*contrasairteevoo*
cream	*pomada*	*poomarda*
diapers	*fraldas*	*fraldash*
disinfectant	*desinfectante*	*desinfairtant*
distilled water	*água destilada*	*argua deshteelarda*
dropper	*conta-gotas*	*conta gotash*
drops	*gotas*	*gotash*
gauze	*gaze*	*garz*
handkerchiefs	*lenços*	*lenssoosh*
healing	*cicatrizante*	*seecatreezant*
injection	*injecção*	*injairsowng*
insulin	*insulina*	*insooleena*
iodine	*iodo*	*eeodoo*
laxative	*laxante*	*lashant*

needle	*agulha*	*agoollea*
oxygenated water	*água oxigenada*	*argua oxeejernarda*
pap	*papa*	*parpa*
pill	*pílula*	*peeloola*
prescription	*receita*	*rersayta*
preservative	*preservativo*	*prerzervateevoo*
sedative	*calmante*	*calmant*
sedative	*sedativo*	*serdateevoo*
sleeping pill	*sonífero*	*sooneeferoo*
sterile	*estéril*	*eshtairil*
sucker	*chupeta*	*shooperta*
suppository	*supositório*	*soopoozeetoreeo*
syringe	*seringa*	*seringa*
tablet	*comprimido*	*compreemeedoo*
tampons	*tampões*	*tampoyns*
tsyrup	*xarope*	*sharorp*
vaseline	*vaesilna*	*verzerleena*
vitamins	*vitaminas*	*veetameenash*

4.3. The human body

Vocabulary

ankle	*calcanhar*	*Calcagnar*
appendix	*apêndice*	*Apendeess*
arm	*braço*	*Brar-ssoo*
armpit	*axila*	*Axeela*
artery	*artéria*	*Artairia*
articulation	*articulação*	*Arteecoolasowng*
back	*costas*	*Corsh-tash*

belly	*ventre*	*Ventre*
bladder	*bexiga*	*Bersheega*
blood	*sangue*	*Sang*
body	*corpo*	*Corpoo*
bone	*osso*	*Ossoo*
bowels	*intestinos*	*Intesh-teenoosh*
brain	*cérebro*	*Sairebroo*
breast	*seio*	*Sayou*
breastbone	*esterno*	*Eshtairnoo*
brow	*sobrancelha*	*Soobransayllea*
buttock	*nádega*	*Nardega*
calf	*barriga da perna*	*Barreega da pairna*
cheek	*bochecha*	*Booshay-sha*
chest	*peito*	*Paytoo*
chin	*queixo*	*Kayshoo*
cranium	*crânio*	*Craneeoo*
diaphragm	*diafragma*	*Deeafrargma*
duodenum	*duodeno*	*Doo-ordairnoo*
ear	*orelha*	*Orairllea*
elbow	*cotovelo*	*Cootooverloo*
esophagus	*esófago*	*Eezorfagoo*
eye	*olho*	*olleo*
face	*rosto*	*Roshtoo*
femur	*fémur*	*Fairmoor*
finger	*dedo*	*Derdoo*
fingernail	*unha*	*Oonha*
foot	*pé*	*Pair*
forehead	*testa*	*Taireshta*
gland	*glândula*	*Glandoola*

gum	gengiva	Jenjeeva
hair	cabelo	Cabearloo
hand	mão	Mowng
head	cabeça	Cabearssa
heart	coração	Coorasowng
hip	anca	Anca
jaw	maxilar	Marxeelar
kidneys	rins	Rinsh
knee	joelho	Joerlloo
leg	perna	Pairna
lip	lábio	Larbeeoo
liver	fígado	Feegadoo
lungs	pulmões	Poolmoynsh
mouth	boca	Boca
muscle	músculo	Moosh-cooloo
nape	nuca	Nooca
navel	umbigo	Oommbeegoo
neck	pescoço	Peshcossoo
nerve	nervo	Nervoo
nervous system	sistema nervoso	Seeshterma nervorzoo
nipple	mamilo	Mameeloo
nose	nariz	Nareesh
organ	órgãos	Orgaownsh
genitals	órgãos genitais	Orgaownsh jenee-tyesh
ovary	ovário	Ovar-reeoo
palate	céu da boca	Saioo da boca
penis	pénis	Pairneesh

ribs	*costelas*	*Coosh-tairlash*
shoulder	*ombro*	*Ombroo*
spine	*coluna vertebral*	*Cooloona verterbral*
skin	*pele*	*Pairll*
spleen	*baço*	*Bar-ssoo*
stomach	*estômago*	*Eshtomago*
tendon	*tendão*	*Tendowng*
thigh	*coxa*	*Cosha*
thorax	*tórax*	*Torax*
throat	*garganta*	*Garganta*
tibia	*tíbia*	*Teebeea*
tongue	*língua*	*Leengooa*
tonsils	*amígdalas*	*Ameeg-dalash*
tooth	*dente*	*Dent*
vagina	*vagina*	*Vageena*
vein	*veia*	*Vaya*
vertebra	*vértebra*	*Vairterbra*
vesicle	*vesícula*	*Verzeecoola*
windpipe	*traqueia*	*Trakayeea*
wrist	*pulso*	*Poolssoo*

Fingers	*Dedos*	*dair-doosh*
index	*indicador*	*Indeecador*
middle	*médio*	*Mairdeeoo*
pinky	*mínimo*	*Meeneemoo*
ring	*anular*	*Anoolar*
thumb	*polegar*	*Poolegar*

5. Time and weather

5.1. Days, weeks, months, calendar

I like the mountains most in the winter.	*É no Inverno que mais gosto da montanha.*	*Air noo invairnoo Ker mysh goshtoo da monta-gna.*
What day is today?	*Que dia é hoje?*	*Ker deea air oije?*
We will leave for the beach July fifth.	*Vamos para a praia a 5 de Julho.*	*Vamoosh Para a pryaa 5 the outoobroo.*
What year did you say you were born?	*Em que ano disseste que nasceste?*	*Ayng ker anoo deessairsht ker nashceshte*
In nineteen eighty-three.	*Em 1983.*	*Ayng meel-nov-centoosh e noventa e traish.*
How old is your father?	*Quantos anos tem o seu pai?*	*Kwantoosh anoosh tayngh oo seoo pie?*
He is sixty-three years old.	*Tem 63 anos.*	*Tayngh sesenta ee traish.*
We leave for summer holiday in three days.	*Dentro de três dias partimos em férias de Verão.*	*Dentroo the traish deash parteemoosh de faireeash the verowng.*
We have an appointment for the dentist next Tuesday at 10 a.m.	*Na próxima terça-feira temos marcação no dentista para as 10 da manhã.*	*Na prorseema terssa fayra termoosh marcasowng noo denteeshta para ash desh da maingnang.*

Time

Spring starts in a month.	*Dentro de um mês começa a Primavera.*	*Dentroo the oom mearsh coomairssa a Preemavera.*
Next autumn, I would like to go to Paris.	*No próximo Outono queria ir a Paris.*	*Noo prorseemoo Outonoo kria eer a pareesh.*
Tomorrow, Sunday, mid afternoon, we'll go to the cinema.	*Amanhã, domingo, vamos ao cinema a meio da tarde.*	*Amaingnang, doomingoo vamoosh ow seenema a mayo da tard.*
Next year, my birthday is on a Wednesday.	*No próximo ano, o dia do meu aniversário é numa quarta-feira.*	*No prorseemoo annoo, o deea doo meoo aneeversario air nooma kwarta fayra.*
I started skiing in the eighty's.	*Comecei a esquiar durante os anos 80.*	*Coomersay a eshkeyar doorant oosh annoosh oytenta.*
Tuesday the thirteenth, like tomorrow, is my lucky day.	*As terças-feiras dia 13, como amanhã, são o meu dia de sorte.*	*Ash terssash fayrash deea 13, comoo amagna, sowng oo meoo deea de sort.*
We are the beginning of the twent first century.	*Estamos no início do século XXI.*	*Eshtamoosh noo ineecioo doo saircooloo veent e oom.*
Next Thursday, I have tickets for the theatre.	*Tenho bilhetes de teatro para a próxima quinta-feira.*	*Tay-gneo beellets the teeartroo para a proseema keenta fayra.*

Vocabulary

afternoon	*tarde*	*Tard*
ages	*era*	*Aira*
age	*época*	*Airpooca*
biennium	*biénio*	*Beeairneeoo*
bimester	*bimestral*	*Beemairshtral*
century	*século*	*Saircooloo*
day	*dia*	*Deea*
day after tomorrow	*depois de amanhã*	*Depoysh the amaingnang*
day before yesterday	*anteontem*	*Anteontain*
dawn	*amanhecer*	*Amagnesear*
decade	*década*	*Dare-cada*
dusk	*entardecer*	*Entardesear*
early morning	*madrugada*	*Madroogarda*
eve	*véspera*	*Vairshpera*
in the morning	*de manhã*	*The maingnang*
leap year	*ano bissexto*	*Annoo beesairshtoo*
midnight	*meia-noite*	*Maya noyt*
milennium	*milénio*	*Meelairneeoo*
month	*mês*	*Mearsh*
night	*noite*	*Noyt*
noon	*meio-dia*	*Mayeeoo deea*
quinquennium	*quinquénio*	*Keen-kwairneeoo*
semester	*semestre*	*Semairshtre*
today	*hoje*	*Oije*
tomorrow	*amanhã*	*amaingnang*
trimester	*trimestre*	*Treemairshtre*
twilight	*crepúsculo*	*Crepooshcooloo*
yesterday	*ontem*	*Ontain*

Week	Semana	semarna
Monday	segunda-feira	Segoonda Fayra
Tuesday	terça-feira	Terssa fayra
Wednesday	quarta-feira	Kwarta fayra
Thursday	quinta-feira	Keenta Fayra
Friday	sexta-feira	Seshta fayra
Saturday	sábado	Sarbadoo
Sunday	domingo	Doomingoo

Months	Meses	mair-zesh
January	Janeiro	Janayroo
February	Fevereiro	Feverayroo
March	Março	Marsso
April	Abril	Abreel
May	Maio	Maeeoo
June	Junho	Joonhoo
July	Julho	Joolhoo
August	Agosto	Agoshtoo
September	Setembro	Sertembroo
October	Outubro	Outoobroo
November	Novembro	Novenbroo
December	Dezembro	Derzembroo

Seasons	Estações do ano	shtasoyngsh
spring	Primavera	Preemavera
summer	Verão	Verowng
autumn	Outono	Outonoo
winter	Inverno	Invairnoo

Time

Era	*Idades*	*Eedadesh*
old age	*Antiguidade*	*Anteegueedad*
middle ages	*Idade Média*	*Eedad mairdeea*
modern age	*Idade Moderna*	*Eedad moodairna*
contemporary age	*Idade Contemporânea*	*Eedad contemporaneea*

Adverbs	*Advérbios*	*ádverbeeoosh*
a while ago	*há pouco*	*are poucoo*
already	*já*	*jar*
always	*sempre*	*sempre*
from time to time	*de vez em quando*	*the vearsh ayng kwandoo*
hardly ever	*de tempos a tempos*	*the tempoosh er tempoosh*
immediately	*imediatamente*	*eemerdeeartament*
in the meantime	*entretanto*	*entretantoo*
later	*depois*	*depoysh*
meanwhile	*enquanto*	*enkwantoo*
never	*jamais, nunca*	*jarmysh, noonca*
now	*agora*	*agora*
often	*frequentemente*	*freekwent-ment*
quickly	*depressa*	*derprairssa*
rarely	*raramente*	*rarament*
right away	*de seguida*	*the segeeda*
sometimes	*às vezes*	*arsh vearzesh*
soon	*em breve*	*ayng brev*
then	*então*	*entowng*
yet	*ainda*	*a-eenda*
while	*enquanto*	*enkooantoo*

Time

5.2. Climate and temperature

It's a sunny day.	*Está um dia solarengo.*	*Eshtar oom deea soolarengoo*
It's cloudy, it will probably rain.	*Está nublado, é provável que chova.*	*Eshtar nooblardoo, air proovarvel ker shova*
Well, as long as it stays like this, we'll have a lot of snow.	*Bem, se continua desta maneira, irá nevar bastante.*	*Bain ser conteenooa deshta manayra, eerar nervar bashtant.*
Do you think it will be cold, hot, where we are going?	*Parece-lhe que estará muito frio, calor, no sítio para onde vamos?*	*Parairsser-ller ker eshtarar moitoo freeoo, calor, noo seeteeoo para ond vamoosh?*
I have opened the windows and it's very sunny.	*Abri as janelas e está um dia de muito sol.*	*Abree ash janairlash ee eshtar oom deea the mooeetoo sol.*
I think that it is going to be cold today and will even rain later.	*Parece-me que hoje fará muito frio, e ainda há-de chover.*	*Parairsser-mer ker oij farar moeetoo freeoo, ee aeenda are the shoovear.*
What will the weather be like tomorrow?	*Como será que vai estar o tempo amanhã?*	*Comooserar ker vye eshtar oo tempoo amaingnang?*
The weather forecast said it would be one degree below zero.	*O boletim meteorológico disse que estará um grau abaixo de zero.*	*Oo boolerteen merteree-oolor-geecoo deesser ker eshtarar oom graoo abyshoo the zairoo.*

air	*ar*	*are*
atmosphere	*atmosfera*	*atmooshfairra*
barometer	*barómetro*	*barormetroo*
climatic	*climático*	*cleemarteecoo*
climatology	*climatologia*	*cleematooloogeea*
cloud	*nuvem*	*noovain*
cold	*frio*	*freeoo*
dew	*orvalho*	*orvarlloo*
downpour	*chuvada*	*shoovarda*
fog	*nevoeiro*	*nevooayroo*
frost	*geada*	*geearda*
frozen	*gelado*	*jelardoo*
hail	*granizo*	*graneezoo*
hailstorm	*saraivada*	*saryvarda*
heat	*quente, calor*	*kiernt, calor*
humidity	*humidade*	*oomeedard*
hurricane	*furacão*	*fooracowng*
ice	*gelo*	*jearloo*
lightning	*relâmpago*	*relampagoo*
rain	*chuva*	*shoova*
raingauge	*pluviómetro*	*plooveeormetroo*
ray	*raio*	*raeeoo*
shade	*sombra*	*sombra*
shower	*aguaceiro*	*arguassayroo*

snow	*neve*	*nairve*
star	*estrela*	*eshtrearla*
storm	*tempestade*	*tempeshtard*
sun	*sol*	*sol*
temperature	*temperatura*	*temperatoora*
thunder	*trovão*	*troovaowng*
wind	*vento*	*ventoo*

Sky	*Céu*	*Sair-oo*
clear	*limpo*	*leempoo*
cloudy	*nublado*	*nooblardoo*
grey	*cinzento*	*sinzentoo*
overcast	*encoberto*	*encoobeartoo*
starry	*estrelado*	*eshtrelardoo*
sunny	*soalheiro*	*sooalhayroo*

Climate	*Clima*	*Klee-ma*
continental	*continental*	*conteenental*
dry	*seco*	*searcoo*
humid	*húmido*	*oomeedoo*
mediterranean	*mediterrânico*	*medeeterraneecoo*
polar	*polar*	*poolar*
rainy	*chuvoso*	*shoovozoo*
temperate	*temperado*	*temperardoo*
tropical	*tropical*	*troopeecal*

5.3. Time

What time do you have, please? What time is it, please?	*Que horas tem, por favor? Que horas são, por favor?*	*Ker orash tayng, poor favor? Ker orash sowng, poor favor?*
It's a quarter to eleven, twenty to, ten to, five to.	*São onze horas menos um quarto, menos vinte, menos dez, menos cinco minutos.*	*Sowng onze orash menoosh oom kwartoo, menoosh veent, menoosh desh, menoosh seenkoo meenootoosh.*
The underground comes every three minutes.	*O metro passa de três em três minutos.*	*Oo metro parssa the trearsh ayng trearsh meenootoosh.*
When should we meet?	*A que horas combinámos encontrar-nos?*	*Er ker orash combeenarmoosh encontrar-noosh?*
In about seven minutes, in a little bit, in less than half an hour.	*Dentro de sete minutos, dentro em pouco, menos de meia hora.*	*Dentroo the set menootoosh, dentro ayng poucoo, menoosh the mayea ora.*
It's eleven o'clock, quarter past eleven, eleven thirty, eleven forty-five.	*São onze horas em ponto, e um quarto, e meia, e três quartos.*	*Sowng onze orash ayng pontoo, ee oom kwartoo, ee mayea, ee trearsh kwartoosh.*
It's almost eleven.	*São quase onze.*	*Sowng kwarze onze.*
In an hour I'll be there.	*Estarei aí dentro de uma hora.*	*Eshtaray aee dentroo the ooma ora.*

It's eleven five, fifteen, twenty, twenty-five, thirty, thirty-five, forty, forty-five, fifty, fifty-five minutes.	São onze e cinco, dez, quinze, vinte, vinte e cinco, trinta, trinta e cinco, quarenta, quarenta e cinco, cinquenta, cinquenta e cinco minutos.	Sowng onze ee seenkoo, desh, keenze, veent, veent ee seenkoo, trinta, trinta ee seenkoo, kwarenta, kwarenta ee seenkoo, sinkwenta, sinkwenta ee seenkoo meenootoosh.
How long before it's finished?	Estará pronto daqui a quanto tempo?	Eshtarar prontoo dakey er kwantoo tempoo?

Vocabulary

at night	de noite	Da noyt
early in the morning	de madrugada	The madroogarda
half an hour	meia hora	Mayea ora
hour	hora	Ora
in the morning	de manhã	The maingnang
in the afternoon	pela tarde	Pella tard
midnight	meia-noite	Mayea noyt
minute	minuto	Meenootoo
quarter of an hour	um quarto de hora	Oom kwartoo the ora
second	segundo	Segoondoo
the middle of the day, midday	meio-dia	Mayeoo deea
three quarters of an hour	três quartos de hora	Trearsh kwartoosh the ora

6. Communication

6.1. Telephone

English	Portuguese	Pronunciation
Where is there a public phone?	*Onde há um telefone público?*	*Ond are oom telefon poobleecoo?*
What area code do I need to call...?	*Que indicativo devo marcar para telefonar para...?*	*Ker indeecateevoo dearvoo marcar para telefoonar para...?*
How does this phone work?	*Como funciona este telefone?*	*Comoo foonseeona eshte telefon?*
What number should I dial?	*Que número devo marcar?*	*Ker noomeroo dearvoo marcar?*
Operator, please connect me to room two thirteen, with extension fifteen.	*Operadora, ligue-me ao quarto número 213, extensão 15.*	*Operadora, Leeger-mer ow kwartoo noomeroo 213 eshtensowng 15.*
You have the wrong number. This isn't it.	*Enganou-se no número de telefone. Não é aqui.*	*Enganor-ser noo noomeroo the telefon. Nowng air akey.*
May I ask who is calling?	*Pode dizer-me quem fala?*	*Pod deezear-mer kain farla?*
Will it take long to connect me to the embassy?	*Demorará muito tempo a entrar em contacto com a embaixada?*	*Demoorarar moitoo tempoo a entrar ayng contartoo com a embaisharda?*

Will you pay for the call or is it a collect call?	*Vai pagar a chamada telefónica ou é a pagar no destinatário?*	*Vye pagar a shamarda teleforneeca or air apagar noo deshteenatario?*
Please, wait a minute, don't hang up, hold the line.	*Espere um momento, por favor, não desligue.*	*Eshpaire oom moomentoo, poor favor, nowng deshleeger.*
Could you speak more slowly, please?	*Pode falar mais devagar, por favor?*	*Pod falar mysh devagar, poor favor?*
He's not here right now, could you call later?	*Ele não está neste momento, pode telefonar mais tarde?*	*El nowng eshtar neshte moomentoo, pod telefoonar mysh tard?*
You could call in fifteen minutes.	*Pode ligar dentro de quinze minutos.*	*Pod leegar dentroo the keenze meenootoosh.*
No answer.	*Ninguém atende.*	*Ningain atend.*
My phone number is...	*O meu número de telefone é o...*	*Oo mearoo noomeroo the telefon air oo...*
Good morning, I would like to speak to information.	*Bom dia, queria falar com a secção de informações.*	*Bom deea, kria falar com a seksowng the infoormasoyns.*
It's connected.	*Está a chamar.*	*Estar a shamar.*

Vocabulary

booth	*cabina*	*cabeena*
conference	*comunicação*	*comooneecasowng*
fax	*fax*	*fax*
headphone	*auscultador*	*aowshcooltador*
mobile	*telemóvel*	*telemovel*
operator	*operadora*	*operadora*
phone guide	*lista telefónica*	*leeshta telefoneeca*
public telephone	*telefone público*	*telefon poobleecoo*
take off the hook	*desligar*	*deshleegar*
telephone	*telefone*	*telefon*
telephon card	*cartão de telefone*	*cartowng the telefon*
to dial	*marcar*	*marcar*
token	*telefone de moedas*	*telefon the mooairdash*

6.2. Communication and the post office

Where is the post office, please?	*Onde ficam os correios, por favor?*	*Ond ficaowng oosh coorayoosh, poor favor?*
Would you give me postage for this envelope, package?	*Queria franquiar este envelope, esta encomenda postal.*	*Kria frankeyar eshte envelop eshta encoomenda pooshtal.*
Where is the mailbox?	*Onde fica o marco do correio?*	*Ond feecar oomarcoo the coorayoo?*

English	Portuguese	Pronunciation
I would like to send this letter certified and next day (urgent). How much is it?	*Queria enviar esta carta registada e urgente. Qual é o preço?*	*Kria enveear eshta carta rergeeshtarda ee oorgent. Kwal air oo prierssoo?*
What window do I need to buy stamps, send certified mail?	*Qual é o guiché dos selos, dos registos?*	*Kwal air oo geesh-air doosh searloosh, doosh rergeeshtoosh?*
I would like to send a telegram. Where is the telegraph office?	*Queria enviar um telegrama. Onde é o serviço telegráfico?*	*Kria enveear oom telegrama. Ond air oo serveessoo telegrarfeecoo?*
I would like to send a telegram, how much do you charge per word?	*Pretendo enviar um telegrama. Quanto cobram por palavra?*	*Pretendoo enveear oomm telegrama. Kwantoo corbraowng poor palarvra?*
I'm here to pick up a money order, telegram.	*Venho levantar um vale postal, telegrama.*	*Vay-gnoo levantar oom val pooshtal, telegrama.*
Is there a letter, money order telegram, in my name?	*Há alguma carta, vale postal, telegrama, em meu nome?*	*Are algooma carta, val pooshtal, telegrama, ayng meoo nom?*

Vocabulary

English	Portuguese	Pronunciation
address	*direcção*	*deeraisowng*
addressee	*destinatário*	*deshteenatareeo*
certified letter	*carta registada*	*carta regeeshtarda*

communication	*comunicação*	*comoo-nee-casowng*
correspondence	*correspondência*	*correshpondencia*
date	*data*	*data*
envelope	*envelope*	*envelop*
letter	*carta*	*carta*
mail	*correio*	*coorayoo*
mailbox	*caixa do correio*	*kysha the coorayoo*
mailed package	*encomenda postal*	*encoomenda pooshtal*
mailing list	*posta-restante*	*poshta-reshtant*
money order	*vale postal*	*val pooshtal*
post office box	*apartado de correios*	*apartardoo the coorayoosh*
postage	*franquia*	*frankeea*
postcard	*postal*	*pooshtal*
postman	*carteiro*	*cartayroo*
printed	*impresso*	*impressoo*
rate	*tarifa*	*tareefa*
receipt	*recibo*	*reseeboo*
redelivery	*devolução*	*dervooloosowng*
remittent	*remetente*	*remetent*
returning	*devolver*	*dervolvere*
sample	*amostra sem valor*	*amoshtra sain valor*
shipping	*envio*	*enveeoo*
stamp	*selo*	*sealoo*

stamped paper	*papel selado*	*papel selardoo*
tax	*taxa*	*tarsha*
telefax	*telefax*	*telefax*
telegram	*telegrama*	*telegrama*
telegraph	*telégrafo*	*telairgrafoo*
urgent	*urgente*	*oorgent*
weight	*peso*	*perzoo*
window	*guiché*	*geesh-air*

6.3. Colours

| What colour is the...? | *De que cor é...?* | *The ker cor air...?* |

Vocabulary

beige	*bege*	*bearje*
black	*preto*	*priertoo*
blond	*loiro*	*loyroo*
blue	*azul*	*azool*
brown, chestnut	*castanho*	*cashtaygno*
chrome	*metalizado*	*metaleezardoo*
colour	*cor*	*cor*
coloured	*colorido*	*coolooreedoo*
dark-skinned	*moreno*	*moorenoo*
flat colour	*cor lisa*	*cor leeza*
florescent	*florescente*	*floreshcent*
green	*verde*	*verede*

Communication

grey	*cinzento*	*seenzentoo*
lilac	*lilás*	*leelarsh*
navy blue	*azul-marinho*	*azool mareenho*
orange	*laranja*	*laranja*
pink	*rosa*	*roza*
purple	*roxo*	*rorshoo*
red	*vermelho*	*vermaylleo*
striped	*às riscas*	*arsh reeshcash*
violet	*violeta*	*veeooletta*
white	*branco*	*brancoo*
yellow	*amarelo*	*amarelloo*

6.4. Numbers and measurements

6.4.1. Numbers

Vocabulary

Cardinales	Cardinais	Car-dee-naeesh
zero	*zero*	*Zairoo*
one	*um*	*Oom*
two	*dois*	*Doysh*
three	*três*	*Trearsh*
four	*quatro*	*Kwartroo*
five	*cinco*	*Seenkoo*
six	*seis*	*Sayesh*
seven	*sete*	*Set*

eight	*oito*	*Oytoo*
nine	*nove*	*Nov*
ten	*dez*	*Desh*
eleven	*onze*	*Onze*
twelve	*doze*	*Dorze*
thirteen	*treze*	*Trearze*
fourteen	*catorze*	*Katorze*
fifteen	*quinze*	*Keenze*
sixteen	*dezasseis*	*Dezasayesh*
seventeen	*dezassete*	*Dezaset*
eighteen	*dezoito*	*Dezoytoo*
nineteen	*dezanove*	*Dezanov*
twenty	*vinte*	*Veent*
thirty	*trinta*	*treen-ta*
forty	*quarenta*	*kwarenta*
fifty	*cinquenta*	*sinkwenta*
sixty	*sessenta*	*sessenta*
seventy	*setenta*	*setenta*
eighty	*oitenta*	*oytenta*
ninety	*noventa*	*noventa*
hundred	*cem*	*sain*
two hundred	*duzentos*	*doozen-toosh*
three hundred	*trezentos*	*trezen-toosh*
four hundred	*quatrocentos*	*kwatroo-sentoosh*
five hundred	*quinhentos*	*keynhen-toosh*
six hundred	*seiscentos*	*sayesh-sentoosh*

seven hundred	*setecentos*	*set-sentoosh*
eight hundred	*oitocentos*	*oyto-sentoosh*
nine hundred	*novecentos*	*nov-sentoosh*
thousand	*mil*	*mill*
two thousand	*dois mil*	*doysh mill*
one million	*um milhão*	*oom meelhowng*

Ordinals	Ordinais	order-nahysh
first	*primeiro*	*Preemayroo*
second	*segundo*	*Segoondoo*
third	*terceiro*	*Tersayro*
fourth	*quarto*	*Kwartoo*
fifth	*quinto*	*Keentoo*
sixth	*sexto*	*Sayshtoo*
seventh	*sétimo*	*Seteemoo*
eighth	*oitavo*	*Oytarvoo*
ninth	*nono*	*Nono*
tenth	*décimo*	*Dareseemoo*
eleventh	*décimo primeiro*	*Dareceemoo-preemayroo*
twelfth	*décimo segundo*	*Dareceemoo-segoondoo*
thirteenth	*décimo terceiro*	*Dareceemoo-tersayroo*
fourteenth	*décimo quarto*	*Dareceemoo-kwartoo*
fifteenth	*décimo quinto*	*Dareceemoo-keentoo*

ommunication

sixteenth	_décimo sexto_	_Dareceemoo-sayeshtoo_
seventeenth	_décimo sétimo_	_Dareceemoo-seteemoo_
eighteenth	_décimo oitavo_	_Dareceemoo-oytarvoo_
nineteenth	_décimo nono_	_Dareceemoo-nono_
twentieth	_vigésimo_	_Veejair-zeemoo_
thirtieth	_trigésimo_	_Treejai-zeemoo_
fortieth	_quadragésimo_	_Kwadre-jairzeemoo_
fiftieth	_quinquagésimo_	_Kinkwajair-zeemoo_
sixtieth	_sexagésimo_	_Sekwajair-zeemoo_
seventieth	_septuagésimo_	_Sairptooa-jairzeemoo_
eightieth	_octagésimo_	_Octajair-zeemoo_
ninetieth	_nonagésimo_	_Nonajair-zeemoo_
hundredth	_centésimo_	_Sentair-zeemoo_

Fractions	_Fracções_	_Frasoynsh_
zero point five	_0,5 zero vírgula cinco_	_0,5 - zairoo veergoola sinkoo_
two point fifty	_2,50 dois vírgula cinquenta_	_2,50 - doysh veergoola seenkwenta_
thirty five percent	_35% trinta e cinco por cento_	_35% - treenta ee seenkoo poor sentoo_
one half	_1/2 um meio_	_1/2 - oom mayo_
one third	_1/3 um terço_	_1/3 - oom tearssoo_
two fourths	_2/4 dois quartos_	_2/4 - Doysh kwartoosh_

mmunication

three fifths	*3/5 três quintos*	*3/5 - Tresh Keentoosh*
two sixths	*2/6 dois sextos*	*2/6 –doysh seshtoosh*
one tenth	*1/10 um décimo*	*1/10- oom dear-seemoo*
addition	*adição*	*Adeesowng*
cuadruple	*quádruplo*	*Kwar-drooploo*
division	*divisão*	*Deevee-sowng*
double	*dobro*	*Dobroo*
dozen	*dúzia*	*Doozeea*
dozen and half	*dúzia e meia*	*Doozeea ee maya*
even	*par*	*Par*
figure	*cifra*	*Seefra*
five times	*quíntuplo*	*Keen-tooploo*
half	*metade*	*Mertarde*
hundred	*centena*	*Sentearna*
multiplication	*multiplicação*	*Mooltee pleecasowng*
one time	*uma vez*	*Ooma vearsh*
pair	*um par*	*Oom par*
percentage	*percentagem*	*Persentar-jane*
subtraction	*subtracção*	*Soobtrar-sowng*
three times	*três vezes*	*Tresh vear-zesh*
triple	*triplo*	*Treeploo*
uneven	*ímpar*	*Impart*

6.4.2. Measurements

The country road is wider after the fifteenth kilometer.	*A estrada regional é mais larga a partir do quilómetro 15.*	*A eshtrarda rergeeonal air mysh larga a parteer doo keelormetroo 15.*
This frame measures three by nine metres.	*Este quadro mede três por nove metros.*	*Eshte kwardroo maird tresh poor nov mairtroosh*
How much does this cheese weigh?	*Quanto pesa este queijo?*	*Kwantoo pairza eshte kayjoo?*
Give me a kilo and a half of fillets.	*Dê-me quilo e meio de filetes.*	*Dear-mer keeloo ee mayo de feeletsh.*
Give me three quarters of a kilo of ham.	*Dê-me setecentos e cinquenta gramas de fiambre.*	*Dear-mer setsentoosh e sinkwenta gramash the feeambre*
What is the area of this piece of land?	*Qual é a superfície desta parcela?*	*Kwal air a sooper-fee-see deshta parsairla.*
What does this door measure?	*Quanto mede esta porta?*	*Kwantoo maird eshta porta?*
How deep is this gallery?	*Que profundidade tem esta galeria?*	*Ker proofoon-deedad tayng eshta galeria?*
How much can this container hold?	*Que capacidade tem este recipiente?*	*Ker capa-seedad taynh eshte rerseepee-ent?*

Vocabulary

Weight	Peso	Pair-soo
fifty grams	cinquenta gramas	sinkwenta grarmash
gram	grama	grammar
gross weight	peso bruto	pairzoo brootoo
half a kilo	meio quilo	mayo keeloo
hangup	tara	tar-ra
hundredweight	quintal	keental
net weight	peso líquido	pairzoo leekeydoo
three quarters of a kilo	setecentos e cinquenta gramas	setsentahs ee sinkwenta gramash
ton	tonelada	toonelarda

Length	Comprimento	Compreementoo
centimeter	centímetro	sentee-mertroo
decimeter	decímetro	dersee-mertroo
depth	profundidade	prorfoon-deedad
height	altura	altoora
kilometer	quilómetro	keylor-mertroo
meter	metro	mairtroo
mile	milha	meelha
millimeter	milímetro	meelee-mertroo
thickness	grossura	groosoors
width	largura	largoora

ommunication

Surface and volume	Superfície e volume	Sueper-fee-see
area	área	areea
cubic centimeter	cm^3 centímetro cúbico	cm3 sentee-mertroo coobeecoo
cubic meter	m^3 metro cúbico	m3 mairtroo coobeecoo
hectare	hectare	airk-tar
square centimeter	cm^2 centímetro quadrado	cm2 sentee-mertroo kwadrardoo
square kilometer	km^2 quilómetro quadrado	km2 keylor-mertroo kwadrardoo
square meter	m^2 metro quadrado	m2 mairtroo kwadrardoo

Capacity	Capacidade	Capasee-dard
half a liter	meio litro	mayo leetroo
hectaliter	hectolitro	• airktor-leetroo
liter	litro	leetroo
quarter of a liter	quarto de litro	kwartoo the leetroo